If Only They Came
with Instructions

A Guide for Parents

Marlene Resnick

"If the children are not protected,

one day

the adults will have to be protected from the children"

from a 1989 report titled:

Suffer the Little

by

Kathleen Brady

Elizabeth Taylor

James Wilworth

About The Author

Marlene Resnick has been a parent educator for over 15 years and a parent for more than 25 years. In the last 5 years she has been a parent educator and more recently a curricula associate for Families First, an organization affiliated with Wheelock College and the Children's Museum in Boston. Before that she directed foster care and counseling programs for 5 years. She was a group therapist for Massachusetts Society for the Prevention of Cruelty to Children where she also provided staff training. She has provided training to the Social Work Training Institute of Massachusetts, as well as, to a number of school systems where she provided training to both parents and staff.

She holds a Masters Degree from Goddard College in Family Studies and was trained at the program on Negotiation at Harvard Law School in mediation, negotiation and facilitation.

Cover: Noah Rosenstein - 18 months old, author's son
Photographer: David Doss
Cover Design: Susan Meyer

ISBN: 0-9650895-0-9

Table of Contents

ACKNOWLEDGEMENTS

There are many individuals to whom I am indebted for their help and support in bringing this book to print. Saf Lerman Caruso, creator of Responsive Parenting, was my first guide in the field of parent education. She provided invaluable tools in the form of her curriculum materials, as well as mentoring me at critical points in my professional development.

The team of parent educators at Families First and Wheelock College Center for Parenting Studies, particularly Phyllis Sonnenschein, Linda Braun and Fran Litman provided support, challenges and opportunities essential in defining and refining my philosophy and ideas.

Frederic Jennings, Jr. made it possible to get the book printed in its initial format on a shoestring. Patsy Ames made the text far more readable and visually appealing through her editing efforts.

Friends Deborah Doss, Judy Solman and Marilyn Meunick helped me to survive financially and emotionally during the writing, rewriting and editing of the manuscript.

My son, Noah Rosenstein and step-daughter Laura Spillane and her son Brendan Spillane have provided great joy, laughter and lessons in abundance. Each has a unique incisive wit, intelligence and personal style that includes empathy and kindness. I thank them for their patience and love during the development of my parenting philosophy.

And last, but in no way least, I owe a debt of gratitude to Edith and Ira Franklin who adopted me when I was in my 30's. They opened their hearts and their home to me and in the process I was reparented.

Issues in Parenting Today

There are some who think that the abuse and neglect of children is the source of our violence domestically, locally, nationally and internationally. Some think that child abuse and neglect are the defining rituals of our society.

I am one of these people.

This workbook is my effort to encourage parents in their own exploration of the parenting adventure. I want to help parents look at what it is we are actually doing with our children — and to see if it is what we *want* to be doing. Are we teaching our children the lessons that we really want them to learn?

The powerful role that parents play in their children's lives is profound and far reaching. We undertake this most important responsibility without instruction or training, sometimes lacking critical information and peaceful problem solving skills.

This workbook tries to provide some much-needed information, ideas, and skills essential for the complex and demanding job of parenthood. As an important part of this process, we will look at what we believe about our job as parents.

There are many books on the "How To" of parenting. They are extremely helpful and a wonderful resource for parents, and, in general, I do not try to duplicate them here. This book was written to encourage discussion and questions about our values and our philosophy in raising our children.

Our society has a history of child rearing which has been punitive and hurtful to children. This history and these actions are based upon a philosophy which has not been challenged in many homes, even today. If we don't confront the problems in this underlying philosophy, we may contribute to the abuse and neglect of our children as individuals, and, as a society, further contribute to the growing violence in our communities.

How this Workbook is Organized

The chapter following this introduction, "A Self Assessment for Parents," gives parents the opportunity for private self assessment. It is critically important to think about what we believe to be our responsibilities as parents, as well as exploring our expectations about our children. If we aren't clear about why we are doing what we are doing, how can it possibly make sense to our children?

The next chapter, "Parenting in a Democracy" explores parenting issues which are unique to families in countries with our type of government. What are the skills which we must teach our children? What are democratic principles, and how are they taught within our families? What do we need to learn, know, and do as responsible citizens of a democracy?

In "Paradigms of Power," we look at some of the concepts of power that are present in our society, and consider the effects they may have on our parenting style.

In "From Paradigm to Principle in Parenting," we look at the outline of both a philosophy and a framework for action that is healthy for children and helpful for parents. The underlying democratic principles involve respect and cooperation, which are essential for all relationships.

If we, as parents, understand how our children learn, we are far more capable of influencing them in their developing values and in their behavior, so another critical need is some information about how children develop and how they learn. "Ages and Stages" provides some information and insight into what issues children are dealing with at different ages. There are certain ages where some forms of difficult behavior actually are "age appropriate."

"Discipline: What Is It, and How Does It Work?" is an important chapter, because discipline is such a misunderstood concept. Discipline situations are often the place where emotions can overtake reason. We, as parents, can harbor a great deal of anger at our own parents, and so may unconsciously take this anger out on our children. This chapter explores the concept of discipline, and distinguishes it from punishment. We will also look at how to deal with difficult behavior more positively, as well as more effectively.

Lack of problem solving skills, often compounded by a history of having been hit or hurt ourselves, can get in the way of handling a discipline situation in ways that are rational and healthy for our children and for us. The powerful emotions of pain and rage will be the focus of the chapter on "Dealing With Emotions: Ours and Theirs." Self esteem, responsibility and cooperation are often defined by the emotional atmosphere of the home environment and the level of respect which individuals experience there.

The final chapter, "Solving Problems Together," focuses on the information and skills needed to solve problems together. Learning how to solve problems in ways that build relationships is the true craft and the ultimate task of parents.

Two Millennia ago ... and Today

Two thousand years ago, it was legal for a husband to kill his wife or children, to sell them into slavery or to treat them in any way he pleased. Today, domestic violence in the form of assault and battery on women and children is common. One in three individuals will witness some form of domestic violence in their homes.

As of this writing, a woman is beaten every 12 seconds in the United States. By the recent statistics it looks as though children are assaulted — hit, hurt, punched, shoved and pulled — every single second. When an adult is hit by another adult, it is punishable by law. As a child, you can be assaulted by someone who may be five times your size and it may be considered appropriate discipline.

When an adult physically assaults another adult, there is no way to interpret that kind of action as discipline. It is assault. With children, we have created a double standard. Until we are willing to bring this issue into focus, we will not be able to understand what action we must take in order to deal with the proliferation of violence in our society.

Punishment vs. Discipline

Discipline and *punishment* are profoundly different ways of dealing with human beings. Discipline is about teaching children what they don't yet know and helping them to learn impulse control. Healthy self esteem is essential for children to develop self discipline. As we feel better about ourselves, we become more able to control our own impulses.

Punishment, however, is based upon pain, either emotional or physical, and is about making us feel bad, which undermines our self esteem, which can lead to the destruction of our self discipline.

Until we separate punishment from discipline in our own minds and our own behaviors we will continue to perpetrate the values of two thousand years ago. This is particularly destructive to a democratic society. We, as American parents, have a real responsibility here.

We need to look at what values punishment creates, recognizing that the home is the place where children learn values. We also need to look at what does and doesn't work, because, in fact, punishment as a form of discipline does not work.

Not only are we as a culture confused about discipline and punishment, but we are also confused about *obedience* and *responsibility.* This confusion causes profound problems within our families and within our communities. If we are not committed to creating an environment where we understand the principles of a democratic social structure, where we can articulate those principles to our children, and where we have respect for those principles in our families, how can we expect our children to understand and embrace them? The issue of discipline — what it is and how it works, and its confusion with punishment — is where our veneer of civilization wears through. Parents are often left with suppressed (or not so suppressed) rage, which can be acted out on those who are smaller, more vulnerable and dependent — children.

The Basic Tools

In my years of working with parents and children, I have come to believe that there is certain basic information and certain parts of their own experience that parents must explore in order to avoid being hurtful to their children.

Parents need a philosophy of parenting based upon principles, an understanding of how children develop physically, intellectually and emotionally, and a knowledge of the difference between discipline and punishment. We need to explore our own childhoods and the feelings associated with our own parents, and our own treatment as children. We need communication skills in solving problems and dealing with difficulties, and we need an understanding of democratic principles and practices.

Without these tools, some parents resort to highly authoritarian measures; others, give up completely and become *laissez-faire* parents. Principled parenting is based upon democratic principles, where children are encouraged to take responsibility for themselves, as soon as they are old enough to do that. And where parents understand that their authority in their role as parent comes from their responsibility to their children — to protect them, to support them and to help them become their own people.

Parents need to have an *expressed* philosophy of their role, their job, and their responsibilities in parenting. They need to explore what they believe about what is important in their relationship with their children. Parents who haven't explored their beliefs generally act out what was taught to them by their parents. Or sometimes, if they really hated what was done to them, they do the exact opposite of what their parents did. Often this happens without the parents having any particular philosophy, and often without their having much understanding of how children learn or much skill in dealing with emotions.

We live in a complicated, difficult and demanding culture. As children, our job is to grow up, to take care of ourselves as well as others, to separate to some degree from our family and to enter the world of work. We live in a culture where there is no welcoming community for our adolescents and young adults. They have to work extremely hard to compete in the marketplace if they can get into it at all.

In both Japan and in Germany, when young people graduate from high school, they are enrolled in job training or college, or they have a job waiting for them. This is an effort that is developed through a coalition among the school system, businesses and the community. Imagine for a moment how different the experience of being welcomed into the adult community must be. They have made a place for you.

We lack this kind of program within our own country. The marketplace does not welcome young people as valued members of the community, but only as consumers.

Why Do We *Punish* Our Children?

If children came with a book of instructions, what would it say? They certainly wouldn't say, "Hit and hurt for improved performance." And yet, this is often how many parents react, creating a hostile and uncooperative atmosphere in many families. Why do we threaten, intimidate, insult or humiliate our children?

The answer always seems to be the same: "That's what my parents did to me" or "What else can you do?"

Many parents find that after they go through the process of exploration, learning, and skill development outlined in this workbook, their children's behavior improves tremendously.

What Are the Options?

We can learn better ways to deal with our children if we want better treatment from them. We know what works. We know that the concepts are pretty simple, although the practice will test our patience and our skill. If we cherish living in a democracy, where freedom goes hand in hand with responsibility, then we need to take responsibility for protecting all children from abuse.

The most effective way to do this, as parents, is to understand clearly what we believe, to look carefully at our own behavior, and to make conscious choices in dealing with our children.

This is a very different response than acting out emotionally, without considering principle or logic.

Learning Cooperative Skills in a Democracy

The social skills of dealing with differences and solving problems, cooperating with others and getting others to cooperate with us, are skills that all children need to learn. Democracy is based upon these skills. But where are these skills being taught?

Undertaking the job of parenthood without understanding our responsibility as citizens of a democratic government and without the skills needed to promote and protect democracy leaves us in grave danger of losing our freedom. This has happened in many neighborhoods, where it isn't safe to be on the streets. The knowledge needed to become a functional, contributing member of the American community is outlined in the Constitution and the Bill of Rights. There has been too little education about these basic American principles within our schools and within our families. Often, when these principles are taught, it may only be in the context of individual rights, without making clear the fact that individual rights rest on each individual being as committed to the same rights for others as he or she is for him or herself.

When Things Go Wrong ...

With a few exceptions, we have not protected our children well in this country, nor throughout the world. We will continue to see the results of this neglect until we place children in higher regard in our culture and in the world. We are living with the results of the application of a philosophy of child rearing which is destructive to human beings. If we want to have any success in reducing violence in our schools, our communities, and our nation and world, we must look first at where violence begins: in our homes.

Creating scapegoats is a natural result of believing in punishment. Violence and addiction are the natural result of punishing, hurting, humiliating, or trying to "control" our children. Unless we grow beyond punishing bad behavior with more bad behavior, what chance do we have of teaching our children anything else?

Until we deal with addiction for what it is — an expression of pain — and until we deal with violence for what it is — an expression of rage — we will be caught up in the wrong paradigm, playing the warrior when nurturing and guidance are what is needed. We can be so busy waging war instead of solving problems that we waste our resources. We spend so much time in battles that we don't have the energy for solutions.

If Only They Came With Instructions ...

The idea of children arriving with instructions is not original to me. If they came with instructions, what would they be?

What do children need when they arrive on this earth, in our families, in our communities? They need nurturance, they need guidance, they need love and affection, they need opportunities for self-expression, and they need a safe environment.

But how, in our culture, are we addressing these needs?

The Results of Neglect, and the Response to It

By the look of the American landscape, we have not provided enough nurture, guidance, love, affection, opportunity for self-expression, or safety for our children. As they act out their responses to neglect and abuse, we see violence and addiction as the major expressions in a culture which has lost its balance and is trying to find itself — through any means necessary.

What is the political response? Punish, hurt, humiliate, incarcerate or kill. This is a Neanderthal response, which exacerbates the underlying problem. This adds abuse to neglect. An eye for an eye and a tooth for a tooth has the net result of leaving everyone toothless and blind. Some of us are deeply scarred. In order to not pass on the neglect and abuse to our children, we must be willing to feel some of the feelings of our childhood again. We must be willing to learn some new information and some new skills. We need to be open to learning from our children and we must have a relatively clear idea of what our job as a parent is.

Why Do Children Have Children?

I once lead a positive parenting series of ten sessions with women who had recently left battering relationships.

As part of one session, I asked them to close their eyes and to think back on their childhood. I wanted them to remember any time that they felt loved, special, or really good about themselves. Their response was shocking and unforgettable.

After several minutes of silence, one by one, each woman said that she could remember nothing that made her feel loved, special, or really good about herself until the birth of her first child, when the she was fifteen or sixteen years old.

Why do children have children? Because children will find a way to get the love they need.

Parenting in a Democracy

What are our beliefs and what are our principles, our values? Do we know? If we do not talk about these issues with our families, with our children, how can they understand what is important to us?

What effect does our raising our children in a country governed by a democracy have on the job of parenting? The underlying concept of democracy is that each person is worthy of respect, no matter how small or powerless. This is, after all, the essence of equality. What skills are needed and how do we teach them to our children in ways that help them get the point of the lesson?

Walk a Mile in My Shoes ...

When my son was fourteen, I slapped his face. I never had hit him before, and when I did, I was appalled and embarrassed. I felt guilty. I had taught parenting education classes. I had run groups. My philosophy was, and is, no hitting and no name calling.

That slap was far more difficult for me to deal with than it was for my son. He says that I didn't hit him very hard and that I was so guilty for so long that he got a lot of mileage out of it.

For me, it signified a failure, a loss, an experience that I needed to learn from.

What I learned was not to be judgmental. We are just human beings and we aren't perfect. We really can't say what we would do in someone else's shoes, or sometimes even in our own, given a volatile combination of circumstances. Parenting is one of the most complicated, difficult and challenging jobs of our life. And future lives depend upon our success in parenting our children.

This workbook is my effort to look at parenting from a perspective that considers the context of family life in a democratic society and to ask the question: What does being a parent mean to me?

There is a great deal of anger at young people for being so violent and irresponsible. But when we take a closer look at some alarming statistics we get a very different view of where the irresponsibility may lie. Sixty-three percent of homicides committed by young people were cases where they killed their mother's batterer. Ninety-one percent of youths involved in the court systems have been raised in the midst of domestic violence.

To cultivate the principles of free speech, we can't slap our children when they say something that we don't like. To cultivate respect, we can't hurt and humiliate. To discourage slander and assault we must stop name calling and hitting.

In order to stop destructive behavior on the part of parents, we need to learn the skills that work. We need to start teaching these practices to ourselves and each other, as if our very lives depended on it. They do.

Where do we begin? With a self assessment for parents.

A Self Assessment for Parents

We begin with a self assessment, not to judge ourselves, but rather to clarify our own beliefs about our job as parents. This is where we see if we are practicing what we preach, and to think about what does and doesn't work in our relationships with our children. In addition, we need to look at our goals as parents, as well as our goals as individuals.

We must explore ourselves, our beliefs, our values, our understandings, and our expectations if we are to build on our strengths and compensate for our weaknesses. We will look at our behavior and see if it is consistent with what we believe. We will look at our expectations of our children's behavior in order to see if those expectations are realistic and age appropriate.

The intent of this chapter is to help parents approach parenting in a way that is not judgmental. So, please, don't focus on what you may have done wrong. We are, after all, only human. We all make mistakes and we will probably continue to make mistakes until we die, because that is one of the most effective ways to learn. Children possess a powerful impulse to grow, and luckily for them and for us, they are quite resilient. In turn, if we want to help our children to learn from their mistakes, then we must treat mistakes as opportunities to learn rather than little nuggets of shame which should be hidden away and denied.

So be gentle with yourself, and remember that this exploration is for you, to help you to identify strengths on which to build and to identify weaknesses for which we can compensate.

NOTE: Each parent should fill out this assessment separately.

Questions for Parents

1. What are my hopes for each of my children?

2. Do I expect my children to be obedient? To "do as they're told," to "behave"?

Are they obedient? *Explain what you mean.*

Are they cooperative? In what ways?

Are they respectful? In what ways?

Are they responsible, given their ages? How so?

3. Do I encourage my children to take responsibility for whatever they may be able to handle? In what ways? *Please think about clothes, food, friends, schoolwork, chores, sleep and self care.*

4. Do I believe in corporal punishment, or hitting, as a form of discipline? Does it work? *Please explain why you think that it works or why it doesn't.*

Are my expectations realistic, age appropriate and healthy for my children and for me?

What are my standards for their behavior based upon?

5. Do I have problems dealing with my anger? What are they?

How do I behave in a conflict situation?

Do I escalate the conflict rather than solve the problem? How?

Do I try to be nice, try to be nice, try to be nice and then explode? What is the process and how does it develop?

Do I:

❑ Nag?

❑ Cajole?

❑ Insult?

❑ Humiliate?

❑ Name call?

❑ Hit or hurt?

Do I tolerate those behaviors from my spouse?

Do I tolerate those behaviors from my children?

Do I set appropriate limits on my children's behavior, firmly and with kindness?

What limits, how and when?

Do I act out of anger rather than taking responsibility creatively for improving the quality of my relationships with my children?

7. What are the most outstanding features of my child's development since his or her last birthday?

How would I describe my children's personalities? *(Give the age and sex of each.)*

What have I noticed about my children's concerns, problems, issues and conflicts at this time?

What concerns me the most about each of my children?

What do I appreciate the most in each one of my children?

Does my child learn best by hearing, seeing or doing; aurally, visually, or kinesthetically? *(For each child.)*

How do my children learn the values that I want to teach them?

8. What do I believe to be my primary responsibility, as a parent?

What are my basic principles about raising my children?

What do I use for guidance?

Am I able to articulate my principles to my children?

What do I tell them about what I believe?

9. Do I treat my children with respect?

    In what ways?

    Am I concerned about being fair or just about enforcing my will?

What are my responsibilities as a parent in teaching my children about living in a democracy?

What are my goals, as a parent?

What are my goals and aspirations for myself, outside of parenting?

How do I feel about myself in my life, beyond parenting?

What are my strengths as a parent?

What are my weaknesses as a parent?

What do I like best about myself?

In what areas would I like to learn or grow?

10. Am I able to see my children as separate individuals who may have ideas, feelings and beliefs which are different from my own?

What are the ways in which my children are most different from me?

For each of those differences, what is most difficult for me to deal with?

For each of those differences, what do I think is most difficult for them to deal with?

Do I listen to my children without always having to judge them or control them?

11. How was I disciplined by my parents?

What do I like about how my parents raised me?

What do I dislike about how my parents raised me?

Do I want to continue the patterns and traditions that I grew up with?

In what ways do I want different patterns and traditions in my family, now?

What am I doing to create those patterns and traditions?

Other thoughts about my parenting style:

Parenting in a Democracy

In any society, parenting is a critically important element in creating the culture. Living in a democratic society demands that we teach democratic principles to our children, and that these principles be articulated, discussed and explored.

What are these principles and what are the skills needed to operate within the parameters of those principles?

In our democracy, the principle of *"of the people, by the people and for the people"* says a great deal in very few words. It means inclusion, consciousness and responsibility. It means that each individual is worthy of respect.

In contrast, we find families where the parents act as feudal lords who hurt and humiliate the children for being disobedient. This leads to anger, resentment and alienation on the part of the child. These are the ingredients which eventually combine to create violence or addiction, or both.

In this environment, children either learn how to fight, which leads to violence, or they learn how to hide, which leads to addiction. These are natural responses for those who are not allowed expression and whose feelings are denied, ignored, or punished. Kids need skills, not punishment. They need to develop empathy, to be loved and guided. Punishment creates alienation, not cooperation. When children who are alienated from their feelings become the standard, the community and the family become a dangerous environment.

Children need to learn to make choices. and the parent's responsibility is to provide those opportunities. Parents often teach children to "do what you're told," when, in fact, what a democratic country needs is parents teaching children responsible action and cooperation.

Children who are manipulated by fear, intimidation, or by hurtful or humiliating "punishments," will, in at least one third of the cases, do something similar to their own children. How we parent our children has a profound effect on how violent a culture we become. Until we are willing to look at the underpinnings of family life through a democratic lens based upon principles of respect and cooperation, I do not believe that we will effectively deal with violence in this country, or the world, for that matter.

"Effective people are not problem minded," says Peter Drucker, "they are opportunity minded. They feed opportunities and starve problems." This is also true of effective parenting.

Parenting in a Democracy: Some Basic Questions

1. What is my responsibility as a parent in a democratic society?

2. What are my underlying principles about parenting in a democracy?

3. What skills do I have to do this?

4. What obstacles do I face in teaching my children about democracy?

Democracy, like responsibility, can't be taught without hands-on experience. Democracy is based upon respect and cooperation. What are the skills needed in order to solve problems and to deal with differences constructively?

Many parent's philosophies are based on the principles of domination and control. This feudal mentality takes its toll. Violence is considered to be the most critical health epidemic by The Center for Disease Control. As of this writing, fifty-five percent of the homicides in this country are committed by friends or family; that is, by people the victim knew. The FBI's statistics indicate that homicide is the second leading cause of death for young people ages 15-24 ... 20,000 per year.

Democracy is not based upon the principles of domination and control. We must take responsibility for teaching our children the basic skills needed to resolve disagreements and deal with differences without violence or slander.

We need to set our energies to this task as an opportunity, rather than a war. Our children are our future life. We need to give them more than slogans, threats, and ultimatums. We need to give them helpful models, to allow for mistakes and to teach respect and cooperation. We need to learn how to set limits on our children's behavior without belittling or attacking them. We need to teach them the skills to get along with others and to take care of themselves. As parents, we are the caretakers of the next generation.

We are often very insistent on our rights to express ourselves, and yet there is often contempt and intolerance for children who want to express themselves. Some parents believe that their children should have no rights in this area. The parents' job is not to silence their children, or only to allow their children to say nice things. In fact, the parents' job is to teach them how to speak freely but responsibly.

Consider these facts.

✓ As of this writing, the fastest growing profession in Massachusetts, this bastion of higher education, is prison guard.

✓ The schools nationwide have witnessed shrinking budgets, while record numbers of prisons have been built.

What are these actions based on? They are based upon the concept of punishment — the fact that we believe that punishment is the way to handle criminals. This has been a very unsuccessful approach and has failed miserably. If it was successful we would have fewer people in prison, not more.

This ineffective belief is not only used to justify building more prisons, but is also often the underlying principle within the family structure. If children misbehave, punish them. When they do what we want them to, reward them. This is an inadequate philosophy with which to rear children.

We have inherited and fought to defend a democratic country, but have hardly treated the native peoples fairly. We have a Constitution and Bill of Rights that, when written, didn't include the Africans who were kidnaped and brought to this country as slaves, women, who were seen as the property of their husbands and fathers, or children, who were property of their parents.

As a democracy we have a good way to go — but we do have principles. For democracy to work, we have to teach our children these principles.

What are our responsibilities in a democracy? Most people think of military obligations, voting and jury duty. To insure the democratic process, we need to teach ourselves and our children how to solve problems and how to deal with differences in ways that improve relationships. We have to learn how to deal with our emotions without resorting to violence, and we have to provide opportunities for our children to become a part of the American culture.

We have to take responsibility for the creation of a culture which welcomes children and take responsibility for a culture in which children have children to be loved. What do we need to do differently to do this?

If children came with instructions, what would they be? The hard part is that we don't know what we don't know. How do we teach what we ourselves haven't learned? We teach principles to our children in words. In action, however, sometimes we threaten, intimidate, insult and humiliate.

And are we aware of what we are doing? I've heard, and hear on a daily basis, lots of indications that parents often do not listen to what their children are saying to them, and are not giving enough thought to what they are saying to their kids.

What are our principles about this, our most important role in the process of evolution? And, as Americans, what do we need to teach our children about how this community, this country, this world works?

Public education was established, in part, for the purpose of the teaching of democratic principles and practices. It was important to the founders of this country that the children should be taught the skills needed to function in a democratic society.

Literacy is a basic requirement, but beyond learning to read and write, there are principles upon which our laws are based which we need to articulate and demonstrate in order for children to understand and participate in a democratic community. Democracy is based upon respect for the individual.

Not only is knowledge necessary, but the development of skills is necessary to function in a democracy. We must be able to solve problems, be creative, be willing to hear all the sides of a problem, and to acknowledge other people's emotions.

The knowledge needed to become a functional, contributing member of the American community is outlined in the Constitution and the Bill of Rights. Often democratic government is interpreted to mean a free market economy and individual rights, but we must not lose sight of the fact that individual rights rest on each individual being committed to the same rights for others as well.

As members of a country with a democratic government, it is our responsibility to teach the skills needed for children of our society to function in a democracy. When the founders of our country established a national educational system, this was why. Literacy is one critical element in teaching children the principles of democracy, and the social skills needed to enjoy their rights and fulfill their responsibilities.

If we invest more heavily in punishment in our families we will see a continued rise in violence and addiction, no matter how many prisons are built or police hired. Will more prisons make us feel safer?

There is ... an artificial aristocracy, founded on wealth and birth, without either virtue or talents ... and provision should be made to prevent its ascendancy....

Thomas Jefferson, 1813

Thomas Jefferson, nearly two hundred years ago, warned against the power of financial wealth. We have allowed the economy to create the values based upon whatever is profitable, and sex and violence sell.

We can't leave the issue of values up to the economy, or the legal system, or the judicial system, or to the educational system, or to religious institutions. Democratic principles must be learned in the family first. But what are these principles?

In America, we are free to believe whatever we want to believe, without interference. We are free to speak, write, publish and lecture on any topic, no matter how controversial. However, we are not free to use intimidation, force or slander. We are not free to infringe upon other people's rights. We are not free to assault other people.

No hitting and no name calling describe our laws, in a nutshell. "Freedom of expression" describes our most basic principle.

Unless we teach these simple democratic values to children in our families, we can not expect them to grow up to understand, value and utilize them later in life.

As citizens of a democracy, not only do we have the right of free speech, we have the responsibility of defending the free speech of others. There seems to be little consciousness of this basic tenet, of this country's foundation, in common culture. The crisis that we are seeing in crime, violence and addiction in this country is a result of our failure to embrace democratic principles ourselves, and our failure to teach them to our children.

This is our failure, and until we are willing to take some responsibility along with our freedom, we can expect to see the continuance of domestic, local and national violence.

Domestic violence, community violence, national violence and international violence all come from the same place. Until we take responsibility for teaching democratic principles and practices in our community and in our families, we will continue to see hate acted out on women, children, strangers and friends, because it was acted out on them when they were children. No army, no police force, and no court system can protect us from ignorance, pain and rage when they come together in an individual or group of individuals. Violence in the community begins with violence in the home. Education of parents and parents-to-be is essential to our freedom and our safety.

Skills in problem solving and dealing with differences need to be learned, practiced and taught. These are the skills that are the "how to" of democracy. The Constitution and the Bill of Rights express the tenets, the beliefs and the principles. The legal and judicial systems handle the situations when problems and conflicts develop. But where do we learn how to treat other people and how to deal with ourselves? We learn that in the first few years of life. We learn that from our parents and siblings, from our primary caretakers. We learn that from how we are treated and how the adults and children around us treat each other.

Democratic principles need to be discussed, utilized and taught within our families and within our schools, if we expect them to be respected, or even understood, within our communities.

Paradigms of Power

*"Things that matter most
must never be at the mercy of
things which matter least"*

Goethe

What guides us in our "rational" decisions? We operate with many paradigms, many of which are unconscious, many of which are so pervasive that we don't even see them.

PARADIGM: *to set up as an example, to show, to model or pattern.*

The legal system's underlying paradigm is an adversarial model. This works quite well in dealing with criminals. However, it is not generally very helpful in dealing with families, particularly for children. During the years in which my work involved spending time in court with adolescents, their parents, their foster parents, the social workers, and the lawyers (at least one to represent the child, the parents, and the state), I was constantly amazed at the insanity, the waste.

I have enormous respect for two particular judges. The first judge said to me, "My area of expertise is law. I'm not an expert in family systems and how they should work. I'm going to rely a lot on the recommendations that come from you and your staff." The second judge said, "I can't make people behave better. All I can do is treat them as criminals. It's not much help for most children."

This paradigm of adversarialism is a very powerful part of the warrior mentality. Right or wrong, win or lose.

Paradigms of Power

Our beliefs lie below the surface of our actions, and they are intimately connected with our emotions. Until we look at the philosophy of parenting in a democratic society and teach democratic principles in dealing with emotions, we will not raise children who have the skills to function successfully in a democratic society.

What are the principles upon which children are parented? Very often, the parent expects the child to be respectful, without having shown the child respect. Often it is the overriding principle of ownership rather than stewardship of the most critical resource a culture has: our children. The parent may want to control the child and may use fear, hurt or humiliation to accomplish this. The parent may then get more and more frustrated at the child's obstinacy or rebellion.

The problem of being in control of your children is that then they don't have to learn to be in control of themselves.

We have confused control with responsibility, fear with respect, power with authority. Until we deal with the philosophical task of separating these concepts, and discussing the responsibilities of parents in raising citizens into a democratic society, we will not deal with the cause of the problems with which we are now faced.

We must also look at the responsibilities of the community and the government. We have left the development of principles to religious institutions and the profit motive. Sex and violence sell, and repression can be profitable, as well.

We are seeing the explosion of this lack of political and social responsibility everywhere in our increasingly violent culture.

Stephen Covey, in *The Seven Habits of Highly Effective People,* says, "Parents are often caught in the wrong paradigm, thinking of control, efficiency and rules instead of direction, purpose and family feeling."

He talks about synergism in nature and how this concept of everything being related to, and necessary to, everything else is also the case in the family. Parenting involves the development of unity and creative thinking with other human beings. This is the real job of parents.

Control is about disunity and the destruction of creativity. It does not help to develop responsibility, respect or cooperation.

We can't parent in a principled way if we are not aware of the paradigms which underlie our actions. The point of looking at paradigms is to look at what beliefs are motivating our action. We don't have to judge our paradigms, but we do need to look at them, to see if what we say and what we do with our children is truly what we mean and what we want to be saying.

We need to develop a new paradigm that involves creativity, nurturance and guidance in our relationships with our children. We need to replace the paradigm of domination and control over children with one that promotes healthy growth for children and parents.

Arno Gruen, in *The Betrayal of the Self,* says:

> *The socialization process can force us into dependency and infantilism. If we are unable to grow out of this, we will yearn to conform to some kind of authority. The central lesson life teaches us is obedience; our behavior is considered desirable if it convinces authority figures of our willingness to be accommodating. The development of an amoral and unthinking attitude of mutual affirmation is the result."*

Operational Paradigms

Operational paradigms are models, patterns or examples from which we operate. There are two main kinds: institutional and personal.

Institutional paradigms are the architects of our psyches in the external world. *Personal paradigms* are the private, intimate models deep within us. These are the models upon which we create the intimate relationships of our lives and upon which we may base our life's work.

Where do we get our paradigms?

We get many of our institutional paradigms from family systems, our nation, the legal system, the business/economic community, religious institutions, and educational institutions.

We develop personal paradigms from cultural, mythical, parental, emotional, spiritual models in our lives.

Let's look at these sources in detail.

Sources of Institutional Paradigms of Power

Institutional paradigms provide us with models for looking at the outside world. To look at ourselves, we need to be able to see the web of beliefs which motivates our actions. We need to look at how the fabric comes together within our society and through us. The act of self examination is totally subjective and is useful as an exercise in and of itself.

We act on the basis of underlying assumptions which are often so deeply ingrained that they are invisible to us. The purpose in looking at these beliefs is not to be judgmental or critical, but to help us to be conscious of and purposeful in what we do or don't do with our children.

It's important to look at our own paradigms, because they are often responsible for the expectations which may fuel our conflicts.

➤ The Family

The family is a multi-generational system that creates itself and recreates itself in the landscape of constantly changing time.

What are the images that we have about families? Our ideas about who a mother should be, who a father should be, and how children should act, all affect the way we treat our children and how we respond to them.

Where did those images come from? Most often they come from our own childhood families, supplemented increasingly from television, movies and other forms of mass media.

These images often come into play in conflict situations.

The family is most often where we learn the roles that we are supposed to play. What do we need to do to get what we want? What we want, as children, is love and approval from our parents. This is what makes us feel welcomed into the family, into the community. This is what gives us to motivation for cooperation and gives us our sense of self esteem.

Think about what your experiences and images of families are.

What does family mean to you?

What scenes or events from your childhood made you feel good about yourself, happy, safe, or loved?

What scenes or events from your childhood made you feel badly about yourself, unhappy, unsafe, or unloved?

If you have answered these questions, you have outlined some of your own paradigms. Does this exploration lead you to thoughts of what you want to do with your children to help them to feel loved, accepted and safe?

➢ *National Paradigms*

In America, rugged individualism and freedom have been the style and the belief which have designed our national character. As a nation, we are rebellious, youthful. and independent. We are proud of our heritage and our democracy.

➢ *Legal Paradigms*

Our legal system is based upon an adversarial model. There is a highly stylized form for the presentation of evidence, for argument and for rebuttal. In the end, one side becomes the winner and the other side, the loser. Fighting against the other side is how you win in the courtroom.

➢ *Business and Economic Paradigms*

The profit motive is the driving force behind the free market economy. Working to make money becomes the way that things get done. It is also the driving force in determining who has the power to do things and what things get done. Money becomes the tool with which material reality is shaped. The basic struggle of life comes down to making a profit. Viability is determined by economics.

➤ Religious Paradigms

The basic religious paradigm of the Western world is monotheism. "There's one God, and He's mine, and male." Obedience is a very large part of all of the monotheistic religions, as well. When there is only one way or one path that is right, those who have a different path cannot help but be seen as wrong. Real life is rarely so black and white.

➤ Educational Paradigms

Children today begin school in the form of day-care at younger and younger ages. The influence of the providers and teachers has an important place in the lives of children.

The older educational model has often been one where the teacher was the dispenser of knowledge and the students absorbed the knowledge through passive listening and repetitive exercises.

This model has changed considerably in recent years. It has been found that children are more effective learners if they are actively involved in the learning process. They also learn better when they teach what they are learning.

At the same time that this improved approach has become available, the schools are becoming more and more crowded, budgets are being cut and teachers are expected to have the same success with larger classrooms but with less in the way of materials and less in the way of supportive social services.

The educational models that represent current thought (interaction, involvement, and participation) provide us with the opportunity to develop abstract thinking skills. Hopefully they also provide us with skills in solving problems and dealing with differences. The examples, the models, the patterns with which we grew up become the future for us, and if we disliked them, we may react against them. The process of becoming an adult is learning to make conscious choices. In order to do that, we must be willing and able to look back from where we came, be willing to face the present and make choices about the future. Nowhere in this society and in the world is this more important than with the parenting, nurturing and protecting of our children.

What are the examples, models and patterns that we are showing our children? Are we telling them that they are only okay if they do what we want them to do? Are we telling them that they need to give up their autonomy in order to be loved? Are we telling them that being obedient is more important than being responsible? These are important questions to ask — and to answer.

Sources of Personal Paradigms of Power

Personal paradigms are our models and examples of respect and cooperation or lack thereof. They are the basis upon which we create our personal relationships or are victimized by them.

Families are the first place we learn about ourselves. They are also the most prominent creator of our personal and institutional paradigms. I have included family in the list of institutional paradigms. Although we may not want to think of ourselves as living in an institution, the family is the oldest institution and the most formative influence in our early years.

➤ Cultural Paradigms

Although "culture" can cover a vast amount of territory, I would like to talk here about culture as the quality of the environment in which we were raised. Were you respected and helped to express and deal with your emotions in a healthy way? Or were you belittled, laughed at and humiliated? What was the emotional flavor of your home? Was it fear of stepping out of line, and not knowing what was in or out of bounds? Were your ideas and thoughts considered, or were you run over roughshod because you were only the child?

What is the atmosphere in your home today? Have you created the same kind of emotional environment that you experienced as a child?

Have you overreacted against your parents in your dealings with your children? For instance, if your parents were highly authoritarian, do you have difficulty setting limits?

Are you able to establish firm yet reasonable boundaries with your children? Are you able to do this in ways that are respectful of them and effective for you?

➤ *Mythic Paradigms*

Cinderella, Snow White, Beauty and the Beast, Roy Rogers, Darth Vader, Prince Charming and Luke Skywalker are just a few models of the paradigms we have seen on television and the silver screen. The media has created various presences which may be as powerful as the family in our early development.

What fantasies are operational for us?

What are our models and roles, and what models and roles are we providing for our children through television, movies and music?

➤ Parental Paradigms

From our parents, we first learn a sense of our worth. If we are valued by our parents from the start, we will always value ourselves and those around us. If we were treated as worthless, a bother, a burden, or a brat, then we may always view ourselves as lacking, not fully formed. In addition, we may try to prove our worthiness to be loved through excelling at our work. Some of the most outstanding achievers have said, "I've spent my life trying to impress my parents and to get their love." Our parents become our first model of how to be in the world, how to get what you want and how to be loved. Our parents teach us how to be responsible and cooperative, respectful of ourselves and others.

What did we learn? And what are we teaching our children? *(Just think about it. Don't judge yourself.)*

➤ Emotional Paradigms

Think about how we learned to react to the world emotionally.

How did we see our parents and our television or movie heroes express their emotions? How did they deal with strong emotions? Was it: "try to be nice" or "blow their heads off"?

Did we as children have healthy ways of dealing with our anger?

Were we allowed to have our feelings? Were we allowed to express our feelings?

Can we express our emotions in healthy ways to our children now?

Do we accept our children's emotions and help them to deal with their emotions in ways that are acceptable to us?

➤ Spiritual Paradigms

Love and acceptance are the central themes in the spiritual life of the child. When the love you receive is based upon performance, and acceptance is based upon playing a role for your parents, the true soul can get lost in the shuffle.

What provides our most important connections in the spiritual realm?

Where do we feel whole and holy?

From Paradigm to Principle in Parenting

Being a parent is one of the hardest jobs in the world. It is also one of the most satisfying. The rewards are love, wonder and insightful lessons. We usually think of parents teaching children lessons, but very often, children have just as many lessons, if not more, to teach their parents.

In order to make choices about what we will do in the future, we need to look at what we are doing now. We can't simply decide not to lose our temper and yell and scream, if that is what we have always done in the past. We must first learn some skills in communicating and problem solving to provide an alternative, because we generally fall back into old patterns unless we have replaced the old patterns with something else. We can't make a proclamation that we aren't going to lose it again, until we have learned new behavior. When we are angry is not the time to try to make changes. The time is when we are calm. Then we can discuss our ideas and beliefs with our children.

We can't suppress our feelings, but we can make choices about how we deal with those feelings. We don't have to *react.* We can *respond.* If it isn't a life- or limb- threatening situation, we can take a moment to step back and take a deep breath and think about what we want to accomplish. Do I want to get my child to bed? Do I want to calm my child down? Do I want to get my teenager to come home on time? Do I want to get my kids to stop fighting with each other? If it is, then fighting with your children won't get you what you want.

If we want respect, cooperation and responsibility from our children, we can adopt some practices which foster these qualities.

The problem is that parents frequently learn some of the techniques but don't change the underlying philosophy of control and domination over children. As a result, basic patterns don't change.

An example of this problem is the practice of using "time-outs." In many instances, adults forget what the purpose is in using a technique if they do not embrace the principle and the reasoning behind the action. Generally, the point of a time-out is to get the child to calm down. The purpose is to provide a change of environment and let the child know that he or she is capable of calming down and that as soon as the child does calm down he or she is welcome back. This is a very different message than, "You're going to sit there for three minutes and think about what you did wrong."

What are the underlying principles with which we parent our children? Principled parenting means that we have principles about what we are doing with our children. These are principles which we believe in, act on, and can articulate to our children.

Principled parenting is about embracing democratic principles. After all, if we expect our children to be capable of functioning in a democracy, they must learn how somewhere.

Democracy is based upon respect for all people. Each of us has a right to that individual respect. Each of our children has a right to that individual respect.

When I talk about democratic principles, I mean the freedom of thought, belief and speech that is guaranteed in the Bill of Rights.

Freedom of speech does not give us the right to slander someone, nor does it give us the right to yell "fire" in a crowded theater. It should, however, mean that we treat thoughts, ideas and beliefs respectfully, including young people's. It should mean that we encourage thinking and questioning. That we respect differences and encourage our children to ask questions and actively look for answers. An example is that of a curfew for young people. Freedom of assembly is a right that adults would not give up easily. Yet for kids, adults react by trying to control rather than encouraging responsibility and self-control. Recently, young people wearing their caps backwards has actually become an issue which parents and other adults have gotten quite upset about.

An adolescent's job is to find out who he or she is, to become an individual outside of the family and to have his or her own identity. As a part of this process, they try on *all* the costumes for *all* the roles. When we as parents don't understand that this is what is going on, this process can be so terrifying that we start trying to control our kids by complaining and nagging, and end up alienating them.

I remember my reaction to my eleven-year-old son's statement, as we got off the Massachusetts Turnpike, that being a toll collector would be the best possible job. It took all my will power to not react to this! Inside I was saying, "Being confined in a little box all day ... freezing hands in the winter ... sweltering in the summer ... being isolated and totally public as well as breathing carbon monoxide all day ... sounds to me like this job is the Career From Hell!"

Instead, I somehow managed to ask him what he thought he would like about the job. He said that he thought that during slow times he could get a lot of reading done, and get paid for it! (There *is* hope — he is in his mid-twenties now, and works in the television industry.)

If we don't understand that our child's job at this stage of development is to find out who he or she is, then we may react from all our own fears and judgments. The natural reaction on the part of a teenager in that situation may be to rebel.

If kids have to separate from their family to have their own identity, they will. If parents can understand the process that their kids are struggling through, and treat their newly developing differences with respect, they will often be surprised at how much more influence they can have on their children. More than anything else, children want their parents' love and acceptance. If parents only show their love and acceptance when children are obedient, they are depriving them of one of the major requirements for healthy self esteem.

If children are loved and accepted even when they are "terrible two's and three's" or the "feisty eleven- to fourteen-year-old" stage, then they go through those stages of development with a sense of respect for themselves. And this is the only thing that keeps adolescents safe at these very difficult and dangerous stages of life.

The strategy of withholding love is not a healthy way to motivate our children into a more cooperative mode of behavior. It has the effect of building resentment, anger and frustration, resulting in alienation and rebellion. We don't have to act pleased with our children when we aren't feeling that way. But we can be loving and accepting of them while setting limits on unacceptable behavior.

This takes a commitment to thoughtful and stable action with our children. It requires us to use impulse control in our behavior. Rather than just reacting emotionally, we have to make a commitment to use our rationality as well. This may sound simple, but it isn't. I have seen parents of many skills and great educational backgrounds disintegrate on the spot when their four- or six-year-old says, "I hate you."

I have seen parents reduced to total embarrassment, frustration and rage by children acting in ways that actually are age appropriate. When parents feel that their job is to control their children rather than to teach their children how to be cooperative and respectful, then they feel a sense of failure when children or teenagers express views differing from their own.

Children learn from their parents. We are models from which they learn either how to yell and scream or how to solve problems — how to enforce their will on others or how to deal with differences in ways that build relationships.

Democratic Principles, Or, "It's My Way or the Highway"

"You don't mean that." "You don't really feel that way." "You're not allowed to say that." "Because I said so." "This is my house and these are my rules."

All of the above statements are examples of behavior that is contrary to democratic principles.

It is a major revelation for some parents when they begin to understand the idea that you learn to be respectful by being treated respectfully, and that you learn how to listen by being listened to.

Practice comes from habit or philosophy, or both. For us to make conscious choices about how to deal with our children, we need to reconsider what we as parents believe our job in raising our children is. I believe that a parents' primary job is to help his or her children to become responsible, self regulating individuals who feel good about themselves.

Our country was based upon principles which respect individual rights and freedom of belief and expression, yet we have had little discussion of what our responsibilities are as parents raising children in a democratic country.

We may hold some truths to be self-evident, but they don't seem to be self-evident in the raising of our children. We must be willing to look at our own principles, and to be able to articulate those principles to our children when they ask us, why?

If we want respect, cooperation and responsibility from our children, we have to be models of such behavior. If we are not respectful of children's ideas, dreams and requests, they do not learn how to be respectful of our ideas, thoughts and requests.

A big part of our job as parents is to set limits on our children's behavior before it is out of control. Our responsibility in this job is to learn how to set limits on children's behavior firmly and with kindness, not out of anger, frustration or a sense of retaliation.

Treating a child's bad behavior with more bad behavior on our part and then expecting the child's behavior to improve is the result of an underlying belief in punishment. This is the belief that when children do bad things, you treat them badly and withhold love and approval, so that they will feel guilty and improve their behavior.

This is, of course, not what happens. When parents punish children, children figure out ways to punish their parents.

Empathy is the emotional basis of morality. If you are hurt, insulted, and humiliated as a child, it may become too painful to feel your own feelings. You become unable to feel for anyone else.

Addiction is the expression of pain. Violence is the expression of rage. Both indicate a lack of impulse control and low self esteem. Regulating drugs and guns won't touch the issue of impulse control. Nor will it address the issues of violence or addiction.

How do we teach our children impulse control? Impulse control is a stage of emotional development which happens as we develop certain skills. It is not necessarily related to intelligence, and varies widely depending on the age or stage of development that the child is in. Self control is the ability to suppress behavior which is destructive or dangerous. Children learn this very slowly. We will discuss this issue more fully in the next chapter, which deals with ages and stages of development.

Whatever the stage of development of our children, we need clear principles concerning the purpose of our job as parents. What are we doing and why are we doing it? What is the purpose of what we are doing? What is the objective in a particular discipline situation? If we are not clear about why we are doing what we are doing, what sense can it make to our children? Also, if we as parents are not clear about our purpose, we often fall back into punitive patterns of behavior which actually work against getting our children to be cooperative and respectful.

Many parents feel that it is their job to keep their kids happy or to control their children. Both of these philosophies have disastrous results. If children are constantly controlled, they don't learn how to take responsibility for controlling themselves. If parents think they have to keep their kids happy, they don't help their kids deal with their feelings. As a result, children never learn how to satisfy themselves.

In order to teach children how to live in a democratic society, we must teach them what democracy means within the family. The only way we can accomplish this is to eliminate hitting and name calling and to educate ourselves about how children actually learn.

We are the models from which our children learn. They learn how to deal with their emotions by watching how we deal with our emotions. If we yell and scream, name call and hit, nag or cajole, this is how we are teaching our children to deal with their emotions.

We provide examples of behavior. Our children learn how to have relationships, how to love and fight, how to share or to hide, and how to deal with stress, conflict and differences.

Ages and Stages: Developmental Milestones

If our job is to teach our children to be responsible, capable individuals who feel good about themselves, we need to understand what patterns of behavior on our part foster these qualities in our children.

Last year, I had the pleasure of meeting a four-year-old who asked why a staff person had left her job. I said: "It's kind of complicated." She said: "OK. Just tell me half."

A couple of years before that, I met a four-year-old whose mother was a client of mine, in group therapy. Upon meeting him, I asked him his age. After he told me his age, he said, "You're real old." Taken aback, I said: "I guess that I am. How old do you think I am?" He looked at me very carefully and said, "Seventeen?"

Then there is the old story of the four-year-old who was drawing a picture in Sunday school. The Sunday school teacher asked, "What are you drawing a picture of?" The four-year-old said, "I'm drawing a picture of God." The teacher said, "But nobody knows what God looks like." The four-year-old, in exasperation, said, "Well, now they do!"

These stories create a composite picture of a four-year-old mind. It is full of answers as well as questions.

Each stage has its own phase of development. When we have a little bit of understanding about what is going in our children's minds, this can help us to teach them information, ideas and values in ways that they can actually understand it. Sometimes we get so focused on teaching our children a lesson that we lose track of the relationship, and we end up teaching a lesson which we never intended to teach. Sometimes this happens because we are trying to teach our children lessons which they are not yet able to learn, because of where they are in their emotional and intellectual development.

Learning a little about the ages and stages of development helps us to cope with our children more from a position of understanding, rather than confusion or projection.

Often, parents interpret their children's behavior from their own position and have little perspective on what the child is trying to do. Most often, the children are just trying to get what they need. That's their job.

Each age and stage has its own beauty and frustration. Understanding this helps us to be better teachers. It also helps our children to become better learners.

In this chapter, I try to present some of the major developmental phases that all children go through one way or another, and to discuss the conflicts and struggles that are a part of each of those stages.

In the Beginning

When children are first born, they feel a part of their mother or primary nurturer. They need to be held, fed, comforted, changed, gazed at and communicated with. They are successful in getting what they need by crying, which is their means of communication.

If the child is healthy, this can still be a trying and stressful time for parents. It is also a period of delight and satisfaction in the growing relationships that develop as the child responds to parents and initiates interaction.

At this point in time, the child doesn't feel like a separate person, except in periods of distress.

When children reach nine or ten months old, suddenly they realize that they are separate human beings. They're amazed. They want to know what it means. They begin getting around and talking and testing every boundary. All of a sudden, parents start saying that their sweet, little, compliant baby is stubborn or has a temper.

Developmentally, the child has realized that he or she is separate from the parent. And realizing that is the beginning of independence. This is what is *supposed* to happen. This is an important stage and the child should not be treated as if he or she is bad. What children need at this stage of development is support in exploring the world within the bounds of safety. Children say *"NO,"* the most powerful word in our vocabulary, between nine and eighteen months old. This is healthy. This is what they are supposed to do then. It means that they now understand that they are separate, can act as individuals, and can express opinions and desires. This is a stage that should be welcomed with acceptance and understanding. Parents, not knowing about the importance of children saying "no," get adversarial and actually start arguing with their toddlers. They often think that their kids are stubborn, or are not listening, or don't respect them as the parents. This generally results in the parent getting angry with the child.

When this happens, the parent often reacts with a punitive attitude. When parents don't understand what is happening developmentally, they don't have the necessary information that they need to respond helpfully.

One to Two

Another very confusing time for parents occurs when children begin to talk. By the time children are three years old they usually are talking in sentences. Parents confuse their verbal acuity with emotional development. This means that although children are talking in sentences and may know the rules in words, their actions are still those of toddlers. They don't have much impulse control.

What is the parents' reaction? Often parents will become enraged, because the child "doesn't listen" to them. Then, the parents may act out their anger on the child. It is critical that parents understand that his type of behavior on the part of two to four-year-olds is normal. Getting into an argument or getting punitive does not help children to develop the impulse control that their parents want of them.

How does impulse control develop? It develops slowly. It develops as parents set limits for children over and over again, until this emotional development takes place.

Hiam Ginott said that you can never win an argument with a child. You can win them over, and you can engage their cooperation, but you can't win an argument with a child. After all, what else do they have to do? We have to go to work, do the dishes, laundry, shopping, and cleaning. What do they have to do? They can argue endlessly.

My own experience with this happened with a one-year-old. She was quite precocious, talking in sentences at that early age, with a pretty impressive vocabulary. We got into an argument and I remember saying to myself, "What am I doing arguing with a one-year-old?"

The answer came to me immediately, "I'm losing." There is no way of arguing with a toddler and winning, so it's best to not argue at all.

Rachel, the one-year-old whom I spoke of, is now in her mid-twenties. I told her that she taught me that lesson and that it was a very important one for me to learn. With toddlers, parents need to remember that they can understand much of what we say to them, but they may not be able to stop themselves, or respond to verbal direction or requests in the way that parents expect.

What parents need to do is to ask their child once or twice for what they want. If the child doesn't respond, then the parent needs to physically guide the child. This should be done before the parent gets angry. It should be done firmly and with kindness.

Very often what happens is that the parent repeats, over and over again, what she wants from her child. The child doesn't do what is being requested and the parent gets angry. This anger often destroys the possibility of engaging the child's cooperation.

Things go wrong, very often, because parents are clueless about what their child is trying to do. So the parent is actually getting angry at the child for something the child can't help — for something that is age appropriate. We shouldn't be angry at our children for not having impulse control. The stage of development between two and four is all about impulse control. They just don't have it. So many times parents have turned adversarial because a two-year-old was just being a two-year-old.

Impulse control is learned slowly, from someone setting limits in a way that is safe and helpful. We do not learn impulse control when someone is whacking or intimidating us. That only teaches us violence or to be sneaky. Self control is, after all, internal. It comes with choices in an environment where we feel safe. It isn't something that a parent can make a child have. When parents get angry and react out of their own anger rather than setting limits firmly and with kindness, the attitude is, oftentimes, punitive. When this happens, parents lose track of what their job is and get lost in their own anger. The result is that the child is hurt or humiliated, made to feel badly. Generally this does not lead to improved behavior from our children. It does not lead to further development of impulse control or a better understanding of the boundaries.

It is critical that we avoid setting up an adversarial relationship with our children. It is important to hear their "no's." It is important that we guide them and teach them, rather than get lost in a conflict of wills from which there are no winners.

If we understand that our child's job is to explore the world from his or her own perspective and that he or she learns in his or her own particular style, at his or her own rate of development, then we won't have unrealistic expectations. If you expect your toddler to have impulse control because he or she apparently says all the right things, you are setting yourself and your child up for great disappointments and frustrations.

When you are aware that they have little or no impulse control, then you won't be angry when you need to step in and assist the child, whether it is with calming down or getting dressed or not hitting. We need to act before we become angry. We can do this while acknowledging their emotions and their opinions. "It's okay for you to be angry, but it isn't okay to hit." "I know you like to stay in your pajamas, but it's time to get changed now."

When a parent says these things, he or she indicates that what the child is feeling is okay. She also indicates that certain behavior is not okay and that she will step in to set limits when the child is out of bounds or needs assistance. This is very important for a child to know. We need to take action. We need to stop the child from hitting, or gently help the child out of pajamas. Many parents resort to yelling, nagging and cajoling, with little success.

For toddlers, the most effective way to proceed is to ask directly for the behavior you want. Ask, if they can do this? If they are unable to do this, then you need to provide physical guidance, follow through in order to help them. Instead of yelling or asking for the third time, try asking once and then if there is no response, get up and take positive, helpful action, not punitive action. Try to stay focused on what you want to accomplish and ask for cooperation. "I really need your help with this. Can you do it?" The answer won't always be "yes." However, you will be surprised at their increased level of cooperation.

You will be surprised by how quickly your children become more respectful. The more times that you repeat yourself, the less influence your words will have. A request, followed by positive, helpful action works in teaching your child what you want him or her to do. It provides the structure and guidance that your child needs in a way that words don't. Children learn kinesthetically. This means that as they go through the physical task with help, they will learn more effectively than if you nag or yell or hit. They learn through doing, not from being told what to do.

Children see themselves through their parents' eyes in their early years. We need to reflect back love and caring, guidance and concern. We need to provide support for independent thoughts and ideas, because that is where children derive their self esteem.

It is also true that the parents' self esteem is an indicator of their children's self esteem. Therefore, improving your own self esteem, as a parent and as an individual, will help your children to have improved self esteem, as well. The years of toddlerhood establish patterns which we deal with for the rest of our lives in our primary relationships about nurturance, independence and self control.

Children need encouragement to explore, express, to learn new skills and to try new things.

When you are about to say "no" or "don't," if it isn't a life- or limb-threatening situation, take a moment to think about giving a choice. Give choices between acceptable behavior, such as, "You can take the ball outside and play with it or you can choose something else to play with in the house." This is very different from saying,"Don't throw the ball inside the house."

Parents need to remember the objective in a situation and not get lost in a battle of wills.

Two to Four

The two- to four-year-old phase is identified by the issue of will power. Impulse control and will power are the inside and the outside of the same skin. In a battle of wills, we do not learn how to solve problems or how to respect limits. We learn how to get what we want at the expense of others, ourselves, our relationships and our self esteem.

The growth that takes place in the first few years of life is unparalleled. The development of language is a highly sophisticated and symbolic art which indicates a giant leap forward for children. Very often children will have a difficult and frustrating time just before major leaps forward in development. This can be seen in both periods of time before walking and talking begin. They can see what they want to do and are frustrated that they can't do it. Then, after their accomplishment of walking or mastering words, they seem to glow. Parents need to understand that self control is a big struggle for children at this stage of life. They do not have full control of their emotions. Parents need to help children to feel okay about themselves and their feelings. They need help in identifying their emotions and help in understanding how to express their emotions.

Biting is an expression of frustration that some toddlers resort to. It can be very difficult and scary. This frustration is usually an expression that comes just before children are able to make themselves understood, or to get what they want.

This is a growth threshold. It is not an indication that your child is mean or bad. He or she will outgrow it. In the meantime, it is important to let the child know that it isn't okay to bite. It is also helpful to acknowledge the child's feeling of anger or frustration and to let the child know other ways that he can express himself.

Four to Six

At four years old the major question is *"why"*? It is a magical age where children want to be engaged in conversation all the time and will often continue to ask "why," because, like the word "no," it is very powerful. It keeps the parent involved in constant conversation.

This is again a time when parents can confuse their children's sophisticated language skills with emotional maturity or intellectual understanding. They can use vocabulary beyond their understanding.

Many parents have a very difficult time with their four to six-year-olds. This is the time of development when gaining independence from parents and friendships with others are most important.

This stage may be typified as loud and is very much a boundary testing phase. Six-year-olds often seem clumsy and slow. A child seems to dawdle partly because this is a time when transitions seem more difficult, because their level of interest in what they do deepens. Often parents say things over and over again but the child is so totally absorbed in what he or she is doing that not a word has been heard.

Six-year-olds truly want to be the center of attention. They can be bossy, demanding and extremely sensitive at the same time. A common picture of a six-year-old is, with hand on hip, "You do this, and this and this." "Okay," you say, "and I would like you to do this, for me, okay?" The six-year-old might respond with, "I'm not your maid."

They have little sense of reciprocity at six years. This often infuriates parents. After a long and trying day of doing all kinds of things that your six-year-old wanted, you make a simple request and she says no. This, too, passes. Parents notice at around seven that children become more responsive and more helpful.

Seven

At seven years old there is often a change in perspective from the six-year-old, "I know everything and can do anything" attitude, to a sense of being a little person in a very big and sometimes scary world.

Fears of death may accompany a more inward, reflective attitude. This age is often an awkward one physically, where children may be missing teeth, may be growing like weeds and may feel extremely self-conscious about their bodies.

This is also an age where children can be thoughtful and considerate. After hearing about this common transition from six to seven, many parents said that they felt very relieved, because they thought that they might have been the cause of their totally confident six-year-olds becoming unsure of themselves and a little frightened by the world at age seven.

Eight

Eight is an expansive age. It seems to be a time when children's ability to deal with abstraction takes a leap beyond material reality. If children are to become collectors, this is the age when they begin to collect things. Children want to know about their heritage; who did they come from and where? They get interested in outer space as well as inner space. Their sense of time expands to the past and future and they are beginning to ask questions about morality and what is right.

Nine and Ten

At nine and ten the moral questions, the questions about what is right or wrong, often become the topic of discussion. This is generally a time of comfortable growth, the calm before the storm. This is often a time of family closeness, when children like to spend time with parents.

Eleven to Fourteen

Eleven is a time of turmoil for many children. Their bodies may be changing and growing too quickly for them to keep up with. I heard a parent describe her adolescents as "hormones with feet." This is often a time of great confusion for kids, as they need to learn how to balance their growth, their new feelings and their increased responsibilities, as they mature into their adult bodies. They become fascinated with becoming a teenager and often take on the roles that they see on television and in the movies. This can be incredibly scary for parents — to see, for example, their innocent young daughter impersonating Madonna, or their son impersonating Michael Jackson.

If parents are able to allow their children to explore, in safety, their interests, without judgment, shame or an attempt to control what the child likes, then the child generally runs pretty quickly through many models of behavior that the parent may find distasteful.

However, if the parent gets fixated on the hair style, backward hat, baggy clothes etc., instead of staying focused on supporting that child in exploration, then often the teenager will become more alienated and rebellious. Adolescence is scary for parent and teenager alike.

Twelve and thirteen is all about friends and relationships, identity. Who am I? What do I believe? Who are my friends and what is important? These are big questions which continue throughout adolescence.

This is an age where children can't stand their parents. Their parents are totally embarrassing to them. And it doesn't matter what you say, or do, because whatever you do it will be the wrong thing. This attitude intensifies at fourteen and often teenagers hit critical mass at this age. When I directed foster care and counseling programs, the fourteenth year seemed to be the age when kids ran away from home or got into trouble with the police.

The years from eleven to fourteen don't *have* to be hellish, but they often are because parents want to control their kids and, as a result, the kids rebel. Cooperation and respect, as well as very clear household rules, need to be established.

These years usher in a whole new level of self control issues that will probably seem a little like two- to four-year-old development. Boundaries, space, loudness, privacy, sexuality and loyalty are all big issues that teenagers are dealing with. They are not easy issues in a society that teaches immediate gratification, communication in sound bites and slogans in place of principles.

Kids have a lot to figure out at this stage of development. A big part of their job at this time in life is to separate emotionally, to some degree, from their family. This is part of the process of teenagers struggling to find out who they are and what their identity is about. In what ways are they special? What is their individual path in life upon this Earth?

If parents are constantly trying to push and shove their teenager into becoming the person they want him or her to be, instead of understanding that this adolescent exploration is part of the adolescent's job, then very often the teenager will crystallize his or her identity around exactly the thing that the parent hates. Survival is risky without good judgment.

What we describe as maturity is the ability to make good decisions, make sound judgments and be responsible and reliable.

The years between eleven to fourteen are difficult for parents because this stage is generally one in which teens are quite self absorbed. They have intelligence and maturity in many ways, but they also may act out in order to test the limits. This stage is a reworking of boundaries, both in terms of space and values.

If parents are not open to this process and end up reducing conflicts to a battle of wills instead of encouraging choices, responsibility and independence, then the teenager will often either rebel or become a skilled liar.

This is a very hard time for parents because early adolescents don't seem to have much empathy with their parents. It is also necessary that they separate, to some degree; this is the job of adolescence. If you have always enjoyed a close relationship with your child, then your child might have to be angry with you in order to initiate that separation. If he or she is very close to you, that process can sometimes hurt. It feels like rejection.

Fifteen

By the time fifteen comes, a sense of responsibility, a new maturity seems to evolve. The total self centered attitude of the fourteen-year-old may begin to show surprising sensitivity and initiative.

At this stage of development, young people have their values and beliefs strongly in place. The skills which they possess in solving problems and dealing with differences are the tools which they need to survive.

Discipline: What Is It, and How Does It Work?

Myths

It's okay to hit kids.

Punishment is an acceptable form of discipline.

The punishment should suit the crime.

It's not good for children to see their parents argue.

Young children can be made to behave.

Children should not be told if their parents are upset, depressed or sad.

Consistency is critical

The parent can control the child.

What are the underlying principles and the underlying experiences that lead to these myths?

We will examine these concepts by taking a look at discipline. What is discipline and how does it develop? We generally hold very strong ideas about why we do what we do with our children. Taking a look at our methods of discipline and the underlying beliefs is essential. It will allow us to fit our beliefs and our actions into an understandable framework from which our children learn what it truly is that we want to teach them.

One of the major reasons that discipline is such a difficult issue for parents is that it frequently gets confused with enforcing the parent's will. It is often totally confused with punishment, which is not at all helpful in the development of cooperation, respect and responsibility.

The confusion is often heightened by parents' not having a clearly defined understanding of what the job is in parenting. To compound matters further, we parents have lots of feelings that we carry around about our own parents, which often come out most strongly in discipline situations with our children.

Remember those myths?

It isn't any more acceptable to hit a child than it is to hit an adult.

Punishment does not teach discipline.

If we see misbehavior as criminal, and treat it as such, we nurture criminal behavior.

Children need to see that their parents can work out disagreements in helpful ways.

Children who are under four years old cannot be made to behave if they lack impulse control. When they are out of bounds, parents should stop in and set limits firmly and with kindness. It is important to act before you get angry.

It is very important to tell your child that you are having a bad day, and that your anger or frustration is not with him or her. Consistency is key, but humanity is more important. Ask yourself what you want to accomplish — acting firmly and with kindness may be more helpful than consistency in some cases.

A parent's job is not to control their children. A parent's job is to keep a child safe and set appropriate limits until children are able to do that themselves. We can engage our children's cooperation successfully, but we are not in control of our children.

What Is Discipline?

The word *discipline* comes from the Latin and means to instruct or teach. *Punishment,* on the other hand, is about inflicting pain or loss.

These are profoundly different philosophies and the difference between them reflects profoundly different values. The strategies of discipline and punishment result in very different behaviors on the part of our children. Discipline is about helping our children develop self control and impulse control, and accepting parental standards, to some degree.

We must generally understand our children's development stages to be able to *discipline* them appropriately. In order for a parent to deal rationally with a fourteen-year-old, for example, the parent needs to understand that his or her child's job, at that stage of development, is to create his or her own identity. If teenagers have to leave the family to be able to express their individuality, they will often do that.

The developing teenager needs respect from parents who also understand that they need to continue to guide, while realizing that the child has many of his or her values internalized by this time. Teenagers are testing the boundaries of what they can do, and much of this is happening out of the parent's sight. My point in talking about a toddler and a teenager is that we must have an operational knowledge of ages and stages of development. If we don't have some understanding of the struggles and challenges that our children are experiencing then we often misunderstand their behaviors and their emotions.

Some parents treat their children like criminals who deserve to be punished because they don't do what is expected. This attitude is one that teaches criminal behavior. Discipline is about guiding our children. This is important for parents to understand. If parents are operating from a punitive attitude, then children don't have a chance to develop their own judgment, which is essential to making responsible decisions. Self-discipline is internal. It isn't something that someone else can do to you or for you. Parents most help, in the development of healthy self-discipline, by encouraging children to make choices and decisions, within the limits of safety. Parents also help most by setting limits on children's behavior when their behavior is out of bounds. Parents have the responsibility of setting those limits firmly and with kindness, not in anger or in retaliation for their own hurt feelings as children.

Self-discipline develops slowly. In the first two to four years, it is really a matter of corrective action. Over and over again, we need to guide children physically, when they are unable to follow through on their own. We need to do this before we get angry, before we have repeated our request more than twice. Discipline is actually a form of nurturance. It is the work of setting limits with children, until they are able to set those limits, safely, themselves.

It is critical that parents learn to carry out this profound responsibility without insulting or injuring children. To do this successfully, we must understand the task, have a philosophy, values that we can articulate to our children about what we are doing and why we are doing it, and have the skills to communicate and solve problems with others, as well as deal with our emotions and our children's emotions in healthy ways.

In short, we must be models for our children in the ways that we deal with conflicts, differences and emotions. If we are yelling, screaming or hitting, then we are teaching our children to deal with their emotions by yelling, screaming and hitting. If we want to teach them better ways to deal with problems in their lives, then we have to act accordingly in our lives.

Why is discipline a difficult issue for parents?

1. Parents are often unclear about what their job is.

2. Parents have unreasonable expectations of their children's behavior due to lack of understanding of stages of development.

3. Parents often carry a great deal of baggage from their own childhoods.

4. Parents are often confused about the difference between discipline and punishment.

5. Parents are often caught in an ineffective paradigm ... trying to control rather than encouraging the development of responsibility.

6. Parents have not necessarily learned how to express themselves in healthy ways. They may lack the communication skills necessary to solve problems and deal with differences.

These are some of the primary reasons that parenting is hard work. It will help us be effective parents if we explore what happened to us as children and remember what that felt like, because these are the feelings that often erupt in discipline situations with our children. We need to tailor our own behavior and our own actions, so that we model what we want from our children.

Discipline is taught by example, as well. Modeling good behavior by solving problems together, instead of fighting, is the most important element. In addition, we need to be clear about what the limits of behavior are and actively step in, when required, to take positive action to guide our children.

We need a new paradigm. Because we often have an ingrained punitive and retaliatory ethic, we may be mired in beliefs that do not solve people problems, and, in fact, are truly destructive to the growth and development of children and teenagers, as well as threatening to basic democratic principles. Enforcing the parent's will ("As long as you're under my roof, you'll live by my rules") and the threat of being hurt, hit, or humiliated to get a child to be respectful or to cooperate are methods mindlessly followed in many households. This never works, in the long run. This kind of belief results in children doing what they are supposed to do only when the parent is watching. This ethic also encourages children to become good liars. It does not help children internalize the values that we want them to learn.

What passes for discipline in many households is in no way related to the development of self-discipline in children. It is the ritual abuse of children as scapegoats for the triggered anger and rage of the parent. It has nothing to do with discipline.

Self-discipline is the process of developing self control and impulse control. It is the process of learning how to cooperate with others. It is the ability to identify and express your emotions, without attacking others. These are skills which are lacking in many families and in many organizations. Using methods of punishment in the mistaken belief that punishment is a form of discipline is the greatest risk to our children's safety and to our children's sense of responsibility. It is the major obstacle to getting our children's respect and the biggest thing interfering with getting our child's cooperation.

How Does Discipline Work?

To help children develop healthy self-discipline it is important to keep our perspective as problem solvers.

Learning how to balance emotion and reason is essential. The way to do this is to be aware of our emotions and aware of our children's emotions. We need to take charge of our behavior, not react emotionally without thinking about purpose, tone and family feeling.

We can't resolve differences if we don't understand them. We need to be reliable and we need to be respectful. We need to be willing to communicate and use persuasion rather than coercion. No matter what our problems or differences with our children happen to be, we must accept them — they are different, unique and worthwhile individuals.

One of the things that parents need to understand is that approval of everything their kids do is not essential to a working relationship. Shared values ("You have to believe just what I believe") may be hard to come by in the adolescent years. If you make the relationship dependent on imposed values ("I won't love you if we don't agree") then your child has no choice but to go underground or rebel when his or her values and beliefs emerge as different from yours during these tumultuous teen years.

We are often focused on the importance of obedience, which is not related to discipline.

In the early years, this emphasis by parents on children being obedient may require their children to give up their autonomy in order to be loved, accepted or possibly even just tolerated. Children, needing their parents' love and acceptance to feel that they have any value, will do whatever it takes to get their parents to be loving, accepting and admiring. This identity is built on "what I do as a child," not on "being accepted for who I am." The abandonment of autonomy to gain a parent's love can the beginning of unhealthy relationship patterns that can last a lifetime.

To help our children to develop healthy self-discipline, we must love them for their uniqueness, their identity and the very special perspective from which they see the world. Our children are in a constant state of flux. It is important to remember that what we identify as stubbornness or rebelliousness is part of the process that children go through. Don't get stuck in the trap of labeling your child stubborn, lazy, or clumsy, because that is how you contribute to making an awkward stage into a lifelong trait.

Children see themselves from their parents' eyes. We have to consciously reflect back acceptance and love for them, even when we set limits on their behavior.

> *Internalization of parental values tends to occur when nurturance and discipline come from the same source. The father who attempts a specialized disciplinary role becomes an alien intruder to his children.*

> *Phillip Slater Footholds*

The mother who attempts to use the father, or some other person, as a disciplinary force, will find that she undermines her own credibility, as well as her children's respect for her.

The core identity of someone who has had to give up autonomy, individuality and uniqueness to be loved, or has had to perform in a certain way to be acceptable, or to do what he or she was told to do in order to be loved, becomes a hungry soul and the path of the hungry soul is to addiction.

A parenting style which attempts to influence children's behavior by withholding love and approval when the children's behavior does not meet with parental standards, creates a core of dissatisfaction with self. Such children generally spend their lives seeking out that love and approval that their parents were unable to give them. Even when they get love and approval they continue to feel that something is wrong inside of them.

We talk about "self esteem" a lot these days. Self esteem is that core identity fabricated from our feelings about ourselves. If our identity, in the early years, is all about what we do, how well we perform, if we have never felt loved and accepted despite our shortcomings and our mistakes, then how can we love and accept ourselves when we fail, or make a mistake?

When our core identity, how we feel about ourselves, is all external, it is out of our control. This is the out-of-control consumer, the addictive personality. When you feel that something is missing, that you always need something else, something new, you are the perfect consumer and the perfect follower. If the approval you got, the love you received, was based upon your doing what you were told by a strong authority figure, you will search for that figure again and again and act out the child's role of submission for approval, like those who follow people like Jim Jones and David Koresh.

In order to help our children develop healthy self-discipline, we must move into a clear understanding of what discipline is and how it works. It must not be about fighting, enforcing one's will, and controlling. It must be about guiding, supporting, loving, nurturing and setting limits firmly and with kindness, when children are out of bounds. It is most importantly about teaching our children what they need to know in order for them to become responsible and capable members of our society.

Many discipline situations turn dangerous when parents are using insult and injury to enforce their will on their child. Of course cooperation can't be enforced. It must be forthcoming. It isn't forthcoming in a situation where a child is being assaulted or insulted. How can it be? Healthy discipline is a form of nurturing, for it helps you to understand the boundaries of safety in your environment. It has nothing to do with punishment and retaliation, and is most effective when not hurtful or humiliating. Many parents believe that their job is to enforce their will upon their children. In fact, the most critical part of a parent's responsibility is to help their children to become independent of them. In essence, a parent's job is to help his or her children develop into self regulating, responsible individuals who feel good about themselves.

If parents feel that their job is to get their children to do what they want them to do, rather than to teach their children how to make decisions and experience the consequences of those decisions, we will see a generation of individuals who are neurotic, rebellious, addictive and/or violent. We are experiencing the results of the belief that enforcing one's will on children is the way to teach them what it is that we want them to learn. In a household where you are valued for what you do and not who you are, deception and dishonesty are cultivated. This also works against developing self discipline.

Families provide the mechanism for children to learn to become functional, responsible people in our culture. Families provide children with much of their self esteem and that level of self esteem is directly related to whether that individual will be violent and hurtful to him or herself or to others, or whether that individual will be a creative, productive and responsible member of society.

How do families contribute to creating a child's self esteem? Healthy self esteem in children correlates with children feeling loved and wanted unconditionally. It also has a lot to do with how children are disciplined. Being a guide who provides a child with safety and opportuny to learn is far more effective in building children's self esteem than hurtful and punishing behavior on the part of a parent.

Self-discipline is, after all, internal; it is about learning self control and being respectful of self and others as well as learning to cooperate. Learning to cooperate means that we have to learn problem solving skills. In many families and on many streets children have only been taught fighting skills. Often, children are not encouraged to use their intelligence, but to do as they are told. Approval and love get mixed up. If children can't fight, then they learn to hide.

Parenting is a complicated and difficult undertaking. The responsibility entailed is enormous. Support is all but lacking; education is minimal. Parents are often isolated with their children and what comes to the surface in parents' actions is how they were treated by their parents when they were children. They may begin to hear themselves say the same words that they heard from their parents and hated as children.

At the other end of the spectrum are parents who hated the way their parents treated them and respond by doing the exact opposite of what their parents did. For instance, someone who had very authoritarian parents may have a problem setting any kind of limits at all.

This problem really needs to be addressed through discussion and action. Discussion with other parents is important, and discussion with children about what your values are is critical if you want your children to have some of your values.

Action is important, because as soon as parents make a healthy change by dealing in more positive ways with discipline situations, they are astounded at how quickly they see a positive response in their children.

An example of this happened in a group of 23 parents that I worked with. These were two-parent, professional families. In most cases, both parents attended. All of the parents had two- to four-year-old children. In our first meeting almost everyone said that they had difficulty getting their children to do what they wanted them to do.

I suggested that during the week parents make an effort to remember to ask their children to do things in a manner that was direct and respectful. If the child did not respond, the parent was to make gentle physical contact, to make eye contact and to say directly to the child, "I really need your cooperation. Can you do that?"

One third of parents in the group used this method during the week. All who tried it were impressed with the simplicity and success of what they had experienced. What was surprising to me, on the other hand, is that they never thought abut asking their children for what they wanted. They had told or demanded they do something. Then they got angry at the children because they responded emotionally, as anyone with a healthy ego would; they were rebellious.

How is it that these very well educated adults did not understand how to get their children to cooperate with them? How is it that they had no idea that two- to four-year-old children don't have much impulse control? How is it that they did not understand that it was their job to teach their children what they haven't learned yet, rather than punishing them for not knowing what they haven't been taught? We as parents must be open to our children and to how they learn. The lack of creativity, compassion and understanding that many parents exhibit in discipline situations with their children often results in children being backed up to the wall. In such situations, children are set up to rebel.

We need to look at discipline situations as opportunities to teach our children what our values are and to help them understand why we believe what we believe. Discipline situations are the best opportunities we have to get our children's trust and understanding.

As parents, it is our job to set limits, firmly and with kindness, when our children are out of bounds. It is also part of the job to be elastic, to expand as our children grow and change. As they become more independent, our role should change. Discipline is about helping children to develop their own impulse control and it is about helping them to deal with their emotions in ways that are not hurtful to themselves and others.

We teach our children self discipline through the self discipline that we exhibit. We teach children to be respectful of us by treating them respectfully and setting limits when children are disrespectful. Often, parents don't ask in understandable language for the behavior they want from their children.

We need to learn how to ask for what we want directly and respectfully with our children. We need to exercise self discipline with our emotions if we expect our children to develop self discipline.

We need to learn how to discipline our children without punishment. In order to do that we need to talk about emotions, because very often parents react emotionally, with little rationality, in discipline situations.

Dealing with Emotions: Ours and Theirs

How we deal with our emotions is generally a combination of many factors in our life; our personality, how emotions were dealt with in our childhood family, how comfortable and accepting we are of the emotions which we feel, and how well our communication skills have developed.

Because we have been reared in families since the beginning of life, the emotional environment of those beginning years has great power in influencing how we deal with our emotions, as well as conflicts and differences. This original emotional environment will be a major contributor to our sense of self esteem.

If we are not able to handle our own emotions in a healthy way, how can we expect our children, who have little experience and less self control, to handle powerful emotions any better than we are able to?

Often, parents try to be nice, try to be nice, try to be nice and then explode. They may justify destructive and childish behavior on their part by blaming the child for acting like a child. If we don't explode, then being nice at all costs leads to pent-up resentment. Being honest and in control of your own behavior works more effectively than trying to be nice all the time.

Some parents are angry most of the time. They feel that they give and give and don't get respect or cooperation from their children.

Some parents get stuck in a parenting role of control, manipulation and performance.

Some parents forget that modeling healthy patterns is not enough. We need to guide our children. We need to *teach* them the skills that they need to deal with emotions in ways that are helpful to them and acceptable to us and our community. Many parents do not understand that this is their most important and critical role. It is important because it will determine the level of self esteem which comes from acceptance of self, self discipline and communication skills.

If I can't express my anger, then it will eventually express itself in a depression within me, or in destructive behaviors toward others. If I can express my anger, then I can grow beyond it — I can transform it. I can learn how to deal with it better, for the next time. If I can't express it, then it grows bigger and bigger and takes up more and more energy to suppress. When we express anger, we need to do it in ways that are not destructive to others, particularly to our children, who are totally dependent upon us. Not only do many parents feel uncomfortable in dealing with their own emotions about a variety of topics, but they are unwilling to hear their children's expression of strong emotions. Parents cringe upon hearing the phrase, "I hate you" from their children. They often respond with, "You don't really feel that way."

Parents who are afraid of their own feelings are unable to hear the expression of rage or pain from their children. When their children try to express these overwhelming feelings, parents often deny them, belittle them or minimize them.

They don't want to see their child in pain, or expressing ugly emotions, so they try to prettify them, ignore them, or sweep them under the rug. Each of these responses sets up a blockade for that child when dealing with his or her emotions.

The most liberating method of dealing with children's feelings is to help them to identify what they are feeling and to help them figure out how to express and deal with those feelings. Denying, prettifying and covering up those feelings can lead to a hungry soul — one who is not seen, not heard, not acknowledged.

In relationships, the big things are actually the little things. Behavior is indicative of our emotional state. How we treat a child's hurt feelings, anger, pain and rage tells them their worth, and is the critical element in the development of a child's self esteem.

When parents try to manipulate the behavior of the child without understanding the underlying emotions, just about everything can backfire. Self mastery and self discipline are the foundations of self esteem and healthy relationships. If, as children, we are told that our feelings don't matter, we are being told that *we* don't matter.

Parenting is a very emotional experience, starting with being handed your newborn child moments after birth. Those emotions form a protective bond between generations that serves the practical purpose of insuring the survival of the species.

Emotions are who we are, how we feel and how we understand and value ourselves. Emotions are about survival. Anger is protective but it can also be dangerous, depending on how we were taught to deal with our feelings. We have a lot of beliefs about feelings that are not discussed very much, but truly need to be in the raising of children.

"I believe that my child is doing this to drive me crazy. He knows just what buttons to push."

This is an example of a belief that some parents have about their particular child. A child's behavior is an important clue to his or her feelings. It is the way that a child attempts to get what he or she need. If the parent is not able to understand that a child's behavior is about getting what he or she needs and reacts from a belief that their child's behavior is a result of evil intent, then he or she is unable to help his or her children get what they want and what they need.

Children are motivated by their emotional needs. "How do I get what I need from my parents and the world? And what do I need to do in return?" This is the motivating force behind children's behavior.

"We have a choice," as Deborah Prothrow-Stith said in a 1994 speech, "Our children are going to get our resources. Do we give them the time and attention, energy and money now, or do we pay about $30,000 per year when they turn into young adults who get sent to jail?"

Being in an environment where it's okay to have your emotions and where the adults around you help you to understand how you are feeling and help you in dealing with difficult emotions is the most critical element in feeling safe and cared for as a child.

It's important to be able to welcome mistakes as opportunities to learn, rather than embarrassments which must be hidden and about which you are encouraged to feel shame. Shame is a frequently used word for many parents. It is an emotion which gets passed through generations, from parent to child. To be made to feel shameful about yourself is another element of the hungry soul. Shame is a sense of outrage within.

Shame-based parenting results in guilt, resentment and anger on the part of the child. This is the motivating force of addiction. Shame-based parenting is based on the underlying assumption that people learn through pain. If a child does something wrong and is hurt for it, then next time the child won't do it. In reality what seems to happen is that children then try to motivate by inflicting pain, as well — if not back onto their parents, then siblings, friends or enemies. Why do so many parents use shame in their attempt to manipulate their children's behavior? Very often, this type of parenting comes from the underlying belief that "My job is to control my child, to mold my child into a vision of my 'should bes' and 'supposed tos'."

Clear communication of honest feelings without attacking or assaulting is not a skill we have learned very well in our families. Many parents forget that children are childish and that they will be for years. They will need to be guided over and over again.

If our major job is to teach our children what they need to know in the realm of emotions and action, then we need to look at what we are saying to them, what we are showing to them in our own actions, in how we deal with difficult emotions. We need to look at how we treat our children's emotions. Can we simply acknowledge our children's emotions, without telling them how they should feel?

Can we respect our children's feelings?

Can we set limits on our children's behavior and still be respectful of their emotions?

The message that is the underlying theme in much of a child's family, community and entertainment existence is that "might makes right." The statistics made public by Murray Strauss in a book titled *Beating the Devil Out of Them* indicate that 90% of American parents are using corporal punishment with toddlers and more than 50% of American parents continue to hit their children into their early teen years.

The violence in our culture comes from those kids hitting back. Our emotions and our communication skills determine the connections that we are able or unable to make with other human beings. The degree to which we are able to identify and experience our emotions is the degree of choice that we have in our actions. We feel a powerful variety of emotions and we have an enormous variety of choices to make in how we react or respond to our emotions. Over thirty years ago Hiam Ginott made a comment to parents who were about to act in anger. He said "Don't just *do* something, *stand* there." His point was, if it isn't a life- or limb-threatening situation, you have a moment to think about what you need to do.

If you are used to acting immediately from your angry feelings, then physically taking a step backwards and taking a breath will help to change your perspective and your bio-rhythms. You can then think about what it is that you want to accomplish in the situation and proceed in that direction, instead of reacting out of your anger.

Emotions are important. All of the emotions that we feel are worthy of attention. But when parents want their children to be happy all the time, they may be unwilling to acknowledge children's anger or pain. A child's anger is as important as his or her joy. Our job, as parents, is to help our children to deal with whatever they feel. It takes time, it takes attention, and it takes a willingness to see your child as a separate human being with his or her own purpose on this earth.

We can help to form that child's character and ultimately, as parents, this is our most important job. We cannot, however, make a child follow our path. Each person has his or her own path on this earth, and our job is to help each of our children to find his unique path, to support and to encourage the development of individual creative spirit.

Character does not develop from people being pushed into a certain mold. Character comes from making real choices in the real world and experiencing the consequences of our choices and actions. A parent's responsibility here is not to a child's happiness, but to a child's *character*. Parents who are constantly busy keeping their children happy may not be able to help children deal with their anger, frustration, fear or pain. If parents feel that they have to do something to make a child happy, they may be helping the child develop the personality of an addict. Parents who are constantly buying things, doing things, feeding things to children when they are upset rather than acknowledging the pain, anger or frustration, contribute to the development of a personality of someone who cannot be satisfied within him or herself.

Just as I was starting to write this chapter, I got a call from a good friend. It was 7:20 AM. She asked if I was doing anything. I said "What's up?" She explained that she was in a crisis with her fifteen-year-old daughter. I told her that I was working on the chapter dealing with emotions, so the call was well timed.

On the surface, the story began with the daughter saying that she couldn't go to a dentist appointment the next day. It was an appointment arranged by the mother. It had escalated into a major family crisis.

The underlying problem turned out to be that the mother's responsibility was to pass on the responsibility for the appointment to the daughter. Instead, she was trying to manage everyone and everything and then being angry and resentful because the daughter was not being responsible.

This is truly the most difficult part of the job of parenting adolescents. The process of letting go is the greatest challenge. This is particularly true when you believe that you have to control everything.

This lesson was taught to me by one client who has two boys who have attention deficit disorder, with hyperactivity. Some of her questions to herself in many situations with her sons are: "In the grand scheme of things, how important is this issue? What difference does it really make? Is anyone going to die if this doesn't get done?"

And my question to her was, "What do you need to do to maintain your balance?" Responsibility cannot be enforced. It is a process, a balance and a transition that is intimately connected with how we teach children to deal with their emotions.

The basic concept that is important here is that if you aren't at home in yourself, you may not be comfortable anywhere. And you can never get enough of what you don't really need. Often parents go to great lengths to avoid facing their children's feelings. And when parents respond to children's emotions by buying them something or feeding them something, they may miss the opportunity to help their children feel good about themselves.

The feeling of being acceptable is connected to feeling that you *are* enough and that you *have* enough, not just in the basic needs of food, clothing and shelter, but also in feeling that you are okay just for being who you are. This is the basis of our self esteem and a sense of our individual worthiness. The hungry soul is the addictive identity, formed around the hole within, where all of the imperfections, faults and inadequate feelings feed off a philosophy of scarcity and defect.

Many parents feel that their job is to whittle their child's ego down to size, make him or her conform to their idea of what a little boy or girl should be.

The job of parenting has to be as elastic as the needs of the children, because the work of parenting is very different from stage to stage. The underlying philosophy, however, needs to be firm and articulatable to children of all ages, throughout the process of parenting.

When children are humiliated and hurt while being commanded to respect and love their parents, what is the lesson that they will learn?

When children have no expression of their pain, suffering or rage, they will eventually re-enact that pain and suffering on others. Often, they will re-enact this humiliation and hurt with their own children. The child who was persecuted becomes the persecutor. You can look to the childhoods of Hitler and Stalin for a couple of examples of children who learned the lessons that their parents taught them. Early debasement and mistreatment of children results in adults who will debase and mistreat others throughout life.

In the arena of emotions, just as in the arena of discipline, we shouldn't punish children for not knowing what they don't know. Our job is to teach them what they need to know. It is a long term process and takes place in the day-to-day relationship of parent and child. Lack of self control in children is part of the developmental process. For parents to be unaware of this is like going out onto the open sea with no life saving equipment. You just aren't prepared for everyday minor incidents, and, as a result, these can, as easily as the wind, turn into major catastrophes. As parents, we are responsible not only for taking care of our children, physically, but we are also responsible for helping them to develop self control. We have a responsibility to help them to identify their emotions and to help them to find ways to deal with those emotions. We all have positive, negative and ambivalent feelings. The healthiest way to deal with emotional problems is to be honest about them.

Many children are bullied out of their feelings by parents who say, "you don't really mean that, you don't really feel that way, you aren't really hungry."

Parents often say these things because they are trying to control their children's behavior by controlling the way their children feel. This strategy does not work.

We often don't understand the meaning of emotions. Anger is a protective emotion. If we have no anger we may not be able to defend ourselves verbally or physically in situations where we need to be able to do that. If parents act as if there is something wrong with the child for having angry feelings, that child is not going to get past feeling that something is wrong with him or her when he or she has such feelings. This style of parenting does not help children deal with their anger or other feelings in ways that are helpful. And, again, it contributes to the development of a personality with the underpinnings of the hungry soul, incapable of being satisfied. We as parents have to accept that children will feel angry from time to time, and that we will feel angry from time to time. We have to be willing to accept the idea that we are all entitled to our feelings without guilt or shame. In addition, we have a right and a responsibility to express our feelings without having to attack our child's person or character.

Powerful feelings cannot be denied, suppressed or made pretty. They must be acknowledged with respect. Sometimes powerful feelings can be diverted, like a river, but they can't be dammed up without eventual overflow. How we choose to deal with our emotions and how we choose to deal with our children's emotions will be an indicator of our child's ability to become a responsible, self-regulating individual.

Responsibility cannot be imposed. It grows from within. It is fed and nurtured by values absorbed in the family and the community. Reverence for life and respect for others' welfare and liberty are the basis for responsible action.

Values cannot be taught directly. They are absorbed and become part of a child through his or her identification with, and emulation of, people who are loved and respected by the child.

> *A war with children cannot be won. Children have more time and energy to resist us, than we have to coerce them. Even if we win a battle and succeed in enforcing our will, they may retaliate by becoming spiritless and neurotic or rebellious and delinquent. The only way to win, is to win them over.*

> Hiam Ginott, *Between Parent and Child*

Character traits cannot be taught in words. They must be demonstrated.

Some of the ways that parents can initiate positive changes in the ways that children deal with their emotions are:

Listen with sensitivity. Have empathy, but don't over-identify. This is how children understand that their feelings are important and that their thoughts and ideas have value. The self worth that develops from being listened to when we are children lasts a lifetime.

State your feelings and thoughts directly, without attacking your child's character or personality. Talk about emotions, yours and theirs, openly. Help children in figuring out what they can do to deal with the feelings that they are having. We need to demonstrate acceptable ways of coping with feelings.

The emotional environment of the household will determine the quality of the relationships that take place therein. The ways in which emotions are dealt with within a household determine the emotional environment. Parents often get into a battle of wills with their children, particularly when children begin to say *"no"* to parents. This often takes place when the child is between fifteen months and two years old.

If parents don't understand what is happening with their child at this point, often a negative and adversarial relationship is developed. Parents can confuse love and approval. As a result, if the child is acting in a way that the parent disapproves of, the parent may withhold love and affection. This establishes a relationship where children have to abandon their autonomy in order to get their parents' love.

This pattern is devastating to healthy development. Children need to be loved and accepted unconditionally in order for them to feel good about themselves. If love and approval are dependent on the child only doing what the parent wants, the child does not have a chance to develop healthy self esteem and independence.

Healthy self esteem and independence are, in fact, the essence of a parent's responsibility. The major paradigm in child rearing is often still based upon the parents enforcing their will on the child, or the other extreme, which is the parents' throwing up their hands and giving up because they feel they have not been successful. In the latter case, this can result in the child becoming a tyrant or being neglected.

Often when children misbehave, parents lose their tempers and justify their loss of control as a reasonable response. This is the result of not having a realistic idea of what children are capable of handling in reaction to their emotional development. In addition, parents may recreate their own experiences with their parents.

As a culture, we are technologically very advanced; however, in our child rearing practices we are often more primitive than what we identify as "primitive" cultures. In simpler cultures, the importance of children is a recognized element in the continuation of the culture. In our very complex, mobile society, children may not have a chance to be connected to an extended family, where there are numerous role models and where diverse people are a part of the family and accepted as individuals.

Although our society is based upon the principles of freedom, this freedom has been extended only to adults. It has not been firmly grounded in responsibility, and, as a result, freedom is often confused with rebellion. If a culture does not create a structure where children are respected and expected to cooperate, where their ideas are important and where they are encouraged to develop their skills so that they can express their individuality comfortably and with confidence, then the culture and society loses that child. There is little welcoming of the child into our culture. Think about our culture. There is a great deal of rhetoric about child welfare, but in fact only a crisis gets attention, and often, not helpful attention. In both Japan and Germany, when students leave high school they are guided into further schooling or training or a job. In this country, if you are not going to college, you receive your diploma and are told "good luck."

If we want our children to be involved in their communities in a positive way, we need to provide the community. We need to establish paths with access to education, training and job placement when they leave school. We need to welcome our young people into the adult world.

Presently, this is not the case. As a result, young people are told to behave, told what not to do, told what to believe, and then, if they are not bound for college, they have the responsibility of entering a job market for which they may not be prepared or skilled enough to obtain employment. Emotions have a great deal to do with how you are or are not accepted into your family and community. Your sense of acceptance, that you are important to other people and you are cared for and that someone is there to set safe limits on you, so that you feel safe and loved, are essential elements for a sense of healthy self esteem.

Emotions are powerful; they define how we feel about ourselves. If we learn how to express our emotions in healthy ways, we are more likely to get what we want, to help others to get what they want and to learn how to solve problems and to deal with differences.

Our issue with violence in this country is not because of guns, though that certainly dramatizes the issue, but rather that violence is still seen as a way to deal with problems.

We need to remember that we are the adults. If we don't like what is happening in our relationship with our child, then it is our job to take creative responsibility to make the relationship better.

In order to do this, we need some basic communication skills beyond listening. We need problem solving skills. We need to be trained in resolving conflicts and dealing with differences.

We need training in this area, because if we don't develop the skills necessary to solve problems, then in a conflict situation we will rely on the power of our will, or the strength of our emotional reaction. Neither is adequate in a situation involving conflict with another person.

In the final chapter of this workbook, we will address the skills needed to communicate effectively, solve problems and deal with differences in ways that are helpful and positive for parents and for children alike.

Solving Problems Together

Most parents, when asked what they want from their children, answer "respect" and "I want them to listen to me."

They don't listen to me.

They don't respect me.

These were the complaints that have come up in every group of parents which I have worked with — from every income level and every educational background.

How do we teach our children to listen?

How do we teach our children to be respectful?

A vast amount of research and my own personal experience indicate the following:

We teach our children to listen by listening to them. We teach our children to be respectful, by treating them respectfully.

We teach our children democratic principles.

Some parents start to get a little nervous, right here. "What do you mean, democracy? Not in my house, I'm the boss." Or, "What do you mean? I do everything for my kids and they still don't respect me. They already have too much power."

We, as a nation of families and communities, are facing a crisis of violence and addiction. We might look to the startling statistics that indicate that 90% of American parents use corporal punishment with their toddlers and more than 50% continue hitting their children into their early teens. Democracy is based upon principles. These are not those principles. Those principles are canonized in our laws, as freedom from assault and slander. Basic household rules of no hitting and no name calling need to be taught in the home, if we ever expect them to be utilized in the community. Democracy means that each individual is entitled to his or her own ideas, beliefs and words, without insult or injury.

In order to be able to teach these principles, parents need to do a little exploration of their own childhood, emotions and beliefs about parenting. In addition, essential information about how children develop, and how they actually learn, need to be understood by parents.

We need a philosophy that we can articulate to our children about what we are doing and why we are doing it. This is how children come to understand how we think about what is important to us. This is the process by which children accept parental standards and values.

We also need to learn the skills of listening and problem solving. We need to learn how to deal with differences in ways that build relationships.

In order to eliminate violence on the streets, we have to eliminate violence in our homes. We must take time to help our children understand how we think and make time to understand and learn about how they think. We need to understand our role and responsibilities as a parent. What exactly is my job with my children?

Parenting involves nurturing and protecting children, while encouraging their growth and independence. It involves teaching them the skills they will need, to live in our society, our world. As parents, we need to be able to set limits firmly and with kindness, as children slowly develop their own impulse control. This job does contain what appear to be contradictions. We receive a brand new human being, who is totally dependent on us for all his or her needs. Our job is to nurture and support that little person, while helping him or her to become independent of us.

So, how is this done?

Let me first tell you where things go wrong.

A two- or three-year-old who is talking in sentences, knows the rules, but continues to break them, such as writing on the wall or hitting another sibling.

What happens?

The parent gets angry because the child *knows* the rule but isn't *listening* or doesn't *respect* the parent. In fact, that isn't the case. Children of two to four have very little impulse control. How well they speak is a function of intellectual development; how well they control their impulses is a function of emotional development.

Children at this age just can't stop themselves sometimes. It has nothing to do with not respecting their parents or not listening to their parents. It has to do with where the child is in his or her development. When parents are ignorant of the fact that a child may understand, but may not yet have the impulse control to be able to stop himself, parents react emotionally, often out of anger. The child is only being age appropriate.

We must understand that the old system of punitive retaliation and punishment gets in the way of teaching children the skills, principles, and values that it is our job, as parents in a democratic society, to teach our children. We must embrace democratic principles and practices, as parents, in order to teach them to our children.

In order to better resolve conflicts with children and teenagers, we need to be willing to look at our own beliefs, behaviors and emotions. Before we can get into the mechanics of resolving conflicts with our children and teenagers, we as parents need to ask some basic questions about what fuels our conflicts. In working with parents and being a parent for a quarter of a century myself, I have come to some conclusions about questions that are critical for parents to explore, if we want to have success in dealing with our children when conflicts arise. And if we want to give them an alternative to violence, we need to give them the tools and the skills to resolve conflicts in ways that improve relationships instead of ways that destroy relationships. These questions are those that you answered in the Self Assessment chapter. They are listed here to refresh your memory.

1. What are my expectations about my children and their behavior?

Do I expect them to be obedient, "Do as you're told," "behave"? Do I encourage my kids to take responsibility for whatever they can handle?

Do I believe in punishment as a form of discipline? Are my expectations realistic, age appropriate, healthy?

2. How do I deal with anger? What do I do in a conflict situation? Do I escalate the conflict rather than solve the problem? Do I try to be nice, try to be nice, try to be nice and then explode? Do I set appropriate limits in ways that teach children what I want them to learn?

3. Do I nag, cajole, insult, humiliate, name call or hit? Do I tolerate those behaviors from my children? Do I tolerate those behaviors from my spouse?

4. Where are my children in their ages and stages of development? How do they learn? How do they learn the values that I want to teach them?

5. What do I believe to be my job as a parent? What do I use for guidance? What is my philosophy? What are my principles? Can I articulate them to my children?

6. Am I concerned about fairness or just enforcing my will? Do I understand, respect and utilize democratic principles in my life, in my family?

7. Am I able to see my children as separate people, who may have ideas, feelings and beliefs different from my own?

8. Am I respectful of my children? Do I consider their ideas, feelings, wishes? Do I listen to my children without having to judge or control their ideas?

9. We also did some exploration of how we felt as children. How were we parented? What did our parents do for discipline? How do I feel about that? What do I like about how my parents treated me? What do I do differently? What patterns do I repeat from my parents, with my children?

In addition to asking those questions, parents must be willing to do some important restructuring work in order to create an environment in which conflicts can be resolved.

1. Creating an atmosphere within which children can express their feelings without fear of reprisal is essential for healthy emotional growth.

2. Having clear and healthy household rules with no hitting and no name calling as boundaries is absolutely essential

to creating a safe environment for children. This is essential for their cooperation and honesty.

If a child is insulted or assaulted, he or she becomes insulting and assaultive, neurotic or psychotic. If a child is insulted or assaulted, why should he or she respect or cooperate with the insulter or assaulter? Many people might answer "fear" to the above question. However, it has been clearly shown that children who are motivated by fear only perform the way they are expected to perform while the person they fear is watching. They don't internalize values in that way. That is not how children learn.

If you have used hitting and name calling as discipline, then you need to sit your children down and tell them that you don't want to do that anymore. You need to let them know that you want to talk about problems and that you will listen to them and that you would like them to listen to you, as well.

Respect and cooperation need to be talked about with children. Democratic principles need to be talked about with children. Let them know that you really need their cooperation and that you want to approach conflicts as problems that can be solved, if you work together, instead of fighting. Ask them if they can agree to no hitting and no name calling as household rules.

Most kids are relieved and a little skeptical. Some parents report dramatic positive changes in their children's attitude, including their being more helpful and cooperative. If they do not agree with the ground rules, ask them why, ask them what they are afraid of and let them know that this is very important to you. Let them know that American law and principle include protection from assault and slander. Simply put, no hitting and no name calling must be first embraced at home, if respect and cooperation is what you want from your children.

Children may test your limits to see if you really mean what you say — if they can trust you. Will you really be respectful and cooperative, or will you lose your temper and resort to yelling, hitting and name calling? We need to model the impulse control that we expect of our toddlers and our teenagers, and stop expecting our toddlers to teenagers to have more impulse control than we do.

In addition to creating a safe environment and having basic ground rules, some areas of confusion need sorting out.

Discipline/punishment

Power/authority

Obedience/ Responsibility

Respect/fear

All the words listed here have tremendous meaning in the raising of our children and yet they are hopelessly confused, one for the other, in all too many family traumas.

Discipline/punishment

To begin with, *discipline* comes from the Latin, meaning to teach. It is about helping children to develop their own impulse control, while setting limits for their protection and the protection of others. It is about helping children take responsibility for their behavior and it's about helping them do it better the next time.

Discipline is how we set limits with our children and try to get children to adopt parental standards, while at the same time encouraging our children to take responsibility for themselves and for their actions.

This is a long, slow process. It takes place in the context of the day to day relationship. Everything doesn't ride on an individual interaction. Discipline is actually a form of nurturance. Healthy discipline encourages mutual respect and cooperation, which is what most parents express wanting from their children.

Punishment, on the other hand, is hurtful to a child's self esteem. The point of punishment is to make the child feel bad, which doesn't help a child to behave better the next time. Punishment sometimes also is a way for parents to act out their own anger on their children without the balance of principle or rationality. If we think about what we are trying to accomplish when we discipline our children, it is generally that we want them to accept our limits and our standards. Punishment does not accomplish this. A punitive attitude makes children feel badly about themselves. When children suffer in self esteem, their development emotionally, physically and behaviorally may deteriorate.

If children have been hit or hurt emotionally, they sometimes feel that they've paid their debt and they are free do to whatever they did again. It becomes a self defeating pattern of fights and arguments that results in bad family feelings of resentment and alienation which results in more bad behavior. These feelings are the underlying motive acted out in violence and addiction. Stephen Covey, in *The Seven Habits of Highly Effective People,* says "Parents are often caught in the wrong paradigm, thinking of control, efficiency and rules instead of direction, purpose and family feeling."

I paraphrase Stephen Covey by saying: the underlying belief in punishment as a form of discipline is like believing that you can use a street map of Boston to find your way around New York City. They just don't relate to each other. What children need to learn better behavior is healthier self esteem, a feeling of being loved and accepted, and someone who will set limits and teach them what they need to learn, without making them feel badly about themselves. When punitive methods are used by parents, it results in increasingly worse behavior on their children's part, creating a downward spiral of discontent. Discipline and punishment are profoundly different ways of dealing with human beings who may have only been on earth, in a family, for a short few years. They don't know the rules and their job is to get what they need. The parent's job is to guide his or her children in developing the skills they will need to survive on their own.

Healthy discipline is about helping children to understand the boundaries of safety in their environment. It is about helping them to understand human interaction in ways that prepare them to be a contributing member of a democratic society. Healthy discipline nurtures the development of self control and impulse control, as well as independence in children.

Violence and addiction are the result of punishing, hurting, humiliating, controlling or neglecting to care for our child population. Until we deal with addiction for what it is: the expression of pain, and until we deal with violence for what it is: the expression of rage, we will be stuck in the wrong paradigm — punitive control and obedience which undermines respect, cooperation and responsibility.

We can't punish bad behavior on our children's part with bad behavior on our part and expect that our children's behavior will improve.

Power/authority

My authority as a parent comes from the responsibility of the role. I am responsible for protecting, nurturing and supporting my children. I am also responsible for encouraging them to become independent, self sufficient adults who are skilled in human relations and are able to become capable members of the community.

Power is about being able to make decisions. This should begin early in life. This is how we learn who we are and what is important to us, as well as how we understand the consequences of our own actions.

Parents can easily confuse power and authority with the excuse of experience, being older and wiser, or of being the adult. Parents need to maintain their authority while encouraging their children to make choices and decisions early. This is how they learn how to make good choices. Children should have the power to investigate their interests and question beliefs.

Obedience/responsibility

I always tell parents that they don't want obedient children. They tend to snicker and say, "Oh yes, I do."

Obedience does not relate to responsibility. We become responsible when we internalize certain values. Parents who demand obedience will find that their children do what they are told while they are being watched, but as soon as the parent is out of sight, so are those values.

How do children become responsible?

It turns out that the development of a sense of responsibility is related to being able to express our emotions. It is not so related to the accomplishment of chores done.

There are numerous examples of meticulous mass murderers, clean and quiet killers. There are examples of neighbors quoted as saying, "He was a nice guy, neat and clean. He kept to himself. We had no idea that he was killing people and burying them in his basement."

Responsibility comes as children make decisions and experience the consequences of those decisions. If parents are making all those decisions for their children, then the children aren't learning the skills that they truly need to learn.

Responsibility grows slowly, as children feel loved for who they are. It develops when parents expect cooperation from their children, model it themselves, and when parents express their appreciation for their children's cooperation.

Respect/fear

Many parents say that they feared and respected their parents — and what's wrong with that? They often comment with frustration that their children aren't afraid of them at all.

Contrary to much popular myth, fear is not the best motivator in a learning situation. It most often raises the stress level, which puts us into a fight-or-flight response. This is good if you have to flee or fight, but it isn't good in a situation where you are supposed to "learn a lesson." Fear gets in the way of processing information and actually slows down the learning process. If I am being attacked physically or verbally, then all of my resources are going into physically and emotionally defending myself. In a situation like that, I'm not available to get the point of the lesson.

Respect is not inborn. Children learn to be respectful by being treated respectfully and understanding that there are boundaries which parents will maintain when children's behavior is out of bounds. Respect comes from being influenceable, from being able to respond, to listen. Parents often find that when they start listening to their children, their children respond in a surprising manner: they start listening to their parents, respecting them more.

Self Esteem

It is very important to talk about self esteem and how it develops. Approximately 80% of the children who enter kindergarten have healthy self esteem. By the time these children get to high school 80% of them have poor self esteem. What is happening to our children?

Healthy self esteem is the foundation upon which our character is built. Healthy self esteem is the foundation upon which we stand, slump or fall.

There is research which clearly indicates that healthy self esteem only develops in an environment where it's okay to have your emotions, to express them and have your feelings acknowledged. And it's where the adults around you protect you and nurture you, where they accept your emotions and help you to express them in appropriate ways, where you are not told how

110

you are supposed to feel, what you can think and what you can say. Research also indicates that punitive treatment of children dramatically diminishes their self esteem, creating resentment and anger. In addition, it raises the stress level and thereby gets in the way of learning.

This combination reduces the child's impulse control, often resulting in a downward spiral into undesirable behavior.

In the many hundreds of parenting groups that I have led, I always ask if people have used spanking as a form of discipline. For those who have, I ask, "Does it work?" The answer is always the same. *No!*

We know what works with children, but in order to implement what works with children, we as parents need to do some very serious exploration of ourselves; we need to open ourselves to learning about children and how they learn, and we need to learn some new skills in listening, respecting, problem solving and dealing with our emotions and our children's emotions.

We need to understand, utilize and teach democratic principles to our children in our homes because, by the time children enter kindergarten, they have already developed their own patterns of behavior, of getting what they need. They come to school, ready to fight or cooperate and learn depending on what they have learned in the first few years, at home.

Remember the importance of humor and empathy.

Humor is the most powerful means of winning children over. Take creative responsibility for making the interaction better. We're the adult. We need to remembers that and act accordingly. Sometimes humor is the best recourse.

Remember your own childhood.

Do you remember the intensity of your feelings? Your children's feelings are as strong and as powerful as your own. Empathy is critical to balance the difficult act of nurturing new life and surviving our own. Sometimes we need to know that there is a difference between a discipline situation and a situation where we need to resolve a conflict. Sometimes we just need to set limits on our children's behavior. We shouldn't be negotiating when a child is out of control. At those times, just set the limit firmly and with kindness.

If you are in a discipline situation with your child, some ways to handle the situation successfully are:

Acknowledge your child's emotions.

Set limits on physical behavior firmly and with kindness.

Stay calm. Separate your emotion from your response.

Instead of saying no, give choices between acceptable behavior.
Redirect attention.

Approach conflicts as problems which can be solved.

Engage children in the process of finding solutions.

Be respectful.

Teach cooperation.

Be willing to laugh and to learn.

Be willing to say you are sorry.

Remember that everything shouldn't be an issue.

Encourage children to make decisions and to experience the results of those decisions within the limits of safety.

Now we are down to the mechanics of resolving conflicts.

What Do We Need to Do in a Conflict Situation?

1. Separate the child from the problem.

Don't lose your temper.

Take a breath. Take a step back and think about what you want to accomplish.

Focus on identifying the problem. Describe it.

No blame, no judgment. State the problem, clearly.

2. Allow children to talk about their feelings.

Talk about your feelings.

3. Ask for cooperation in solving the problem

Brainstorm, think about all the options without judging or deciding.

Get child involved in thinking about solutions.

What else can be done, instead?

4. Sometimes you need to talk about the criteria.
What are the elements of a good solution?

5. Choose a solution together.

How will this work? Who needs to do what?

In order to follow these simple five steps we often need to do some other things which parents may not find as easy, and that involve a change in our attitude if we have been punitive, controlling, or have given up and have children who walk all over us. The list is as follows.

1. We need self control in dealing with our own emotions.

2. We need a willingness to listen to all sides.

3. We need a willingness to express our emotions without hurting or humiliating practices.

4. We need to eliminate blaming, name calling and hitting if we have been using those strategies of frustration.

5. We need to learn how to accept our children's emotions and to acknowledge them, even when we have to set limits on their behavior.

6. We need to help our children to express their emotions in ways that are healthy for them and acceptable to us.

7. We need a willingness to deal with differences as problems which can be solved rather than fights which must be won.

8. We need to learn to be inclusive and creative in problem solving.

9. We need to understand that fighting and arguing are not helpful ways to deal with conflicts. We need to learn the skills of problem solving and teach them to our children.

The process of solving problems together will not only help to improve your relationship with your children, but will help you in dealing with differences and in resolving conflicts in other relationships, as well. When parents begin the process of solving problems with children, rather than trying to control their emotions and behavior, self esteem grows for both parent and child. In addition, children learn responsibility. The ability to respond is the polar opposite of obedience. The ability to respond is the act of becoming responsible. Let's make sure that we are teaching our children what we really want them to learn.

"Your workbook is terrific and is very compatible with the philosophy of nurturing."

Dr. Stephen J. Bavolek
Founder of The Nurturing Programs

"You have conceptualized critical issues in a clear and very useful way. It is really valuable and should be aggressively marketed."
Dr. Ruth Borofsky

"A gem on every page"
Marybeth Pereira

"Wherever I opened the book, I found little nuggets of wisdom."
Frederic Jennings Jr.

"Your book was critical for us at this time with our kids. It is well organized and explained. Thank you."
Roberto Chau

If Only They Came with Instructions

A Guide for Parents

Marlene Resnick

Please send _____ copies to:

Name:_____

Addresss:_____

City, state, zip:_____

Please mail your order to: Training and Education Resources, 500 South Washington Drive, Suite 16B, Sarasota, FL 34236. Phone: 941-388-6415.

Please include a check for $25.00 per copy plus shipping and handling. (Shipping and handling: $5.00 for the first copy and $2.00 s/h for each additional copy shipped to the same address.)